Preface

The educational potential of computer tools or applications in our class-rooms has been well aired. We have a good impression of what we think can be achieved – even though there are several competing realities – but to what extent have these ideas been put into practice? Have class-room teachers grasped the ideas of the theorists and implemented them with gusto, or is there an unbridgeable gulf between potential and practice? Clearly, our ideas of the potential have not been fully implemented. One of the aims of this book is to identify common problems of innovation, as well as highlighting successful implementations. An important element of the book is the mechanism to capture the day-to-day experience of practising classroom teachers and set that in a theoretical framework.

We have taken several generic applications, such as word processing packages, and outlined the potential for each as an amplifier and as catalyst for educational progress. Following a description of each application there follows a small number of case studies which describe how the packages have been used in the classroom and a description of the educational outcomes. Each of the applications is tied to one or more of the following National Curriculum Strands: Communication, Information Handling, Modelling, and Measurement and Control.

We hope that this book will stimulate those teachers and teachers in training who lack confidence in the use of technology, or have yet to see its relevance in their work, to take a step into the technological classroom. Equally the organisational issues raised by the teachers, for example the lack of high-quality hardware to support the software advances, should provide food for thought for curriculum planners and hardware and software designers.

Jean D. M. Underwood
University of Leicester

Chapter 1

Introduction: *1989 - more computers in school*
Where are we now and where are we
going? *way/ returning to the question again*
can computer age ... " is the growth of
computer usage in schools ... simply a case
Jean Underwood *of technological bandwagon or a genuine*
educational

Writing in 1989 we asked the question whether the growth of computer
usage in schools was simply a case of a technological bandwagon or a
genuine educational opportunity (Underwood and Underwood, 1990).
We quoted Patrick Suppes' 1966 prediction that educational computer
usage would change the face of education in a very short space of time.
A prediction still to be met when Seymour Papert (1980) expressed his
ambitious aims for classroom computers. The machine that would allow
us to abandon the worksheet curriculum and confidently allow children's minds to develop through the exploration of computer simulated
'microworlds'. At that time we said that though there was evidence of a
significant impact of micro-technology in some areas of our educational
system these prophecies remain just that.

It is perhaps not surprising that 5 years on the position remains much
the same. There are some high spots but limited overall penetration.
Even Seymour Papert (1994) starts his latest book by pointing out just
how resistant to change education has been. He tells the tale of a party
of teachers and surgeons travelling forward in time from a previous
century:

> 'each group is eager to see how things have changed in their profession a
> hundred or more years into the future. Imagine the bewilderment of the
> surgeons finding themselves in the operating theatre of a modern hospital ...
> in almost all cases they would be unable to figure out what the surgeon was
> trying to accomplish. The time travelling teacher ... might be puzzled by a
> few strange objects ... but they would fully see the point of what was being
> attempted and could easily take over the class' (p. 1).

Adults born before either of the World Wars would find little difficulty
in understanding the activities of current schools and classrooms but a

pre-First World War factory worker would find the *mores* of a modern car plant mystifying, as would an Edwardian surgeon entering a modern operating theatre. And far from getting rid of worksheets, the computer – that most modern device – is actively placing them back in the classroom through the use of tutoring systems.

Is this resistance to change a cause for concern? Perhaps we should consider first what we are trying to achieve when we send our children to school.

Promoting useful learning

The practice of education is a complex event but the goals of education are deceptively simple. I try to emphasise to the student teachers I work with that our main role is to promote useful learning. Teachers are involved in the social and moral development of the children in their care but they share these goals with many others, such as parents, peers, social workers, youth workers and the police. Indeed the social and moral development of the child is primarily, although not exclusively, the responsibility of the parent. The primary responsibility of the teacher is to encourage the cognitive development of the child, to ensure the retention, understanding and active use of knowledge and skills. As David Perkins (1992) asks, what is the point of acquiring knowledge if it is not to be retained? What is the value of knowledge if we don't understand it? What purpose is there to knowledge that cannot be used in studying other subjects or in 'out-of-school' environments now and in later in life?

These seemingly simple goals have proved remarkably elusive. We fail to achieve even the simple goal of knowledge retention over any significant period of time. Ask any new graduate 6 months after their final degree how much they retain of their course. They always display a frightening degree of information loss, whether through failed retention or an inability to generate an effective retrieval cue.

When we look at learners' understanding of knowledge the picture is even more bleak. There are often profound misunderstandings of key concepts of the subject domain. The focus on knowledge retention is all too visible in our education system; understanding and application have long been subsidiary goals. John Bransford (1989) and his co-workers have highlighted the problem of the vast store of 'inert knowledge' which learners hold passively but which they cannot use in any real context. Information Technology (IT) skills at first sight have that real-world relevance and our knowledge of IT is 'obviously' applied – isn't it? Ron Ragsdale (1991), for one, would argue that this is not the case.

Working with Canadian Teacher Trainees, he has shown that acquiring IT tool skills may be relatively easy but gaining the wisdom to use them effectively may not! IT is a classic area of the curriculum where we need to aid learners in effective use of their knowledge.

How should we teach learners to learn? Do current theories help us towards our key educational goals of the retention, understanding and application of knowledge?

Models of learning

Current educational thinking supports three models of learning, each of which is good in a specific area: the constructionist model for formal conceptual learning; the apprenticeship model for skills development; and the behaviourist model for the passing on of large bodies of structured material. Beverly Woolf's position on educational theory and learning encapsulates the current debate:

> 'I hold a rather eclectic position on learning and cognition ... a constructionist view for concept learning, a situated view for apprenticeship learning and a behaviourist view for classification learning. One model of learning is too constraining.'

> (Barnard and Sandberg, 1992, p.148)

The constructionist view is that knowledge is in the learner's head. Such learning is epitomised by the classic Piagetian (1952) model incorporating the dual processes of assimilation of and accommodation to new knowledge. Assimilation is the addition of non-conflicting knowledge into previously developed cognitive schemas. Accommodation takes place when new knowledge challenges and forces a reshaping of those schemas. This is essentially a conflict-based mechanism of learning in which the learner takes elements from the environment and incorporates them into his or her own model. Vygotsky's (1978) concept of the 'zone of proximal development' and Schank's (Barnard and Sandberg, 1992) concept of 'failure-driven learning' are also related to learning at the point of conflict although here the learner develops through guided intervention. The 'zone of proximal development' refers to that stage in the development of a skill or ability that lies between the learner functioning independently and functioning with support. Schank argues it as this point of failure that teacher (or machine) intervention is most effective. Wood (1988) describes such intervention as contingent teaching, providing support as the learner has need of it rather than teaching in advance of need. Here the notion of discovery learning has evolved into the concept of guided discovery but the central tenet that the construction of knowledge occurs through the process of challenge to existing understanding remains.

Situated learning, the second of Woolf's models, suggests that knowledge is found in the environment, that it is always relative and open to interpretation, and that people can only learn within a culture. Knowledge is within the culture and is open to debate and reinterpretation. To gain that knowledge the learner must be active in the community and come to share the values and *mores* of the society in order to acquire the assumptions necessary to understand the new knowledge. The learner is situated in the learning environment and becomes involved in 'legitimate peripheral participation' acquiring knowledge through the handling of artefacts and listening to 'stories' of how things have been solved in the past (Lave and Wenger, 1991). A process by which learners become part of a community of practice.

This is essentially an 'apprenticeship' model of learning and may be the most appropriate way of acquiring a skill such as making an omelette or learning to drive a car. It is also the currently 'favoured' method of training the teaching profession in England and Wales, and in this case the community is the school. To learn an abstract concept such as 'force', however, requires that the learner resolves misconceptions and clarifies parameters. Such formal concepts are not 'encultured'; they are not held within the student body, for example. They are not negotiable – rather they require a re-construction of knowledge by the learner.

The behaviourist model of learning emphasises the learner's responsiveness to relationships between stimulus events and their consequences, at the expense of any acknowledgement of the learner's understanding or other mental states. Here the teacher or the world has the knowledge and will communicate it to the student. This is standard form of learning in subjects such as geology or medicine where taxonomies, large bodies of structured information, need to absorbed by the learner without any reconstruction of the data. In learning such classificatory systems some repetition of examples is required until the learner changes behaviour or knowledge in response to the represented stimulus. The chosen examples must provide both typical and outlying or extreme examples to allow the boundaries of the classification to be established.

Each of the three models of learning is good in a specific area: the constructionist model for formal conceptual learning; the apprenticeship model for skills development; and the behaviourist model for the passing on of large bodies of structured material. Should we be concerned that we have no one unifying theory of learning? Woolf would argue not, citing the need for more than one theory of physics.

Newtonian theory can explain 'everyday' motion but not the motion of small particles or motion at high velocities. Here the theory of quantum mechanics is required. It is not that any one model of learning is wrong, rather that each may prove to be appropriate in different situations.

Resource limitations, apart from any educational considerations, preclude the provision of a computer for each individual student, and so we must consider the shared use of machines in co-operative learning situations. Co-operative learning refers to learning environments in which small groups of students work together to achieve a common goal.

The social underpinning of co-operative learning emphasises that learning under positive contact conditions can facilitate interpersonal relationships which may in turn have positive effects on student motivation, self-esteem and academic learning. Such positive effects have been shown across all age ranges, ethnic groups, classes and abilities. The cognitive view of co-operative learning emphasises cognitive interactions such as conflict resolution, cognitive scaffolding, reciprocal peer tutoring and overt execution of cognitive and meta-cognitive processes and modelling. This is an argument taken up again in Chapter 2 where we find that boys, girls and computers are a dangerous combination.

IT is capable of supporting each of these models of learning. IT skills themselves are often best taught through the apprenticeship model. Frustrating hours can be saved if the learner has a mentor to come to his or her aid at a critical point, for example when the computer seems unable to find the printer. Acquiring problem-checking routines from an 'expert' is the method by which most of us have learnt to cope with the machine. Trying to decipher such routines from the manual can be soul-destroying!

The computer is also an effective programmed learning box presenting and re-presenting learners with a body of knowledge to acquire. Equally, however, the computer is able to act as a problem setter presenting the learner with cognitive conflicts such as a world without gravity, or an encrypted text passage (see Chapter 2) which the learner, or preferably learners, must endeavour to make sense of and incorporate into their understanding of their world.

What is the nature of the effect of IT on teaching and learning?

 'Almost any form of human cognition requires one to deal productively and imaginatively with some technology. To attempt to characterise intelligence independently of those technologies seems to be a fundamental error.'

(Olson , 1986, p. 356)

6

The early 1980s were dominated by a perception that classroom IT must be doing good and little or no evaluation took place. Richard Clark (1983) led the assault on this new faith criticising those who 'knew IT did you good' but saving his most damning attacks for those conducting low-quality research. He argued that every positive effect attributed to IT would be better attributed to such factors as the quality of teacher input, novelty or motivation of the students. These criticisms lead to a more rigorous empirical evaluation of the classroom IT. Our own work (Underwood, 1986; Underwood and Underwood, 1990) and that of say Klahr and Carver (1988) showed that there were measurable learning gains though the use of IT. There was, however, considerable evidence, particular in the study of LOGO, of the ineffectiveness of IT strategies.

The contradictions in the evidence set the next research question 'Under what conditions is IT beneficial to learning?' For example, Wishart and Canter (1988) investigated the relationship between cognitive demand, motivation and learning in computer simulations. She found that children responded to both an increased level of control and to challenge or cognitive demand. Control may also be seen in terms of ownership – a significant factor in the successful use of IT that we return to in Chapter 6. Although many have said computers are for boys (see Chapter 9) meta-analyses of the gender, attitude and IT competence literature reveals that although boys are more likely to be more enthusiastic about computers, this gender bias disappears if girls see the relevance of computing and, in particular, if their first experience of the computer is not through programming sessions.

- IT can have beneficial effects on teaching and learning.
- Not all use of IT will lead to educational gains.

IT, under the right conditions, can have an effect on teaching and learning but what is the nature of that effect? There have been several papers published discussing this question. Rushby (1979), after Kemmis, established a categorisation of software that implicitly explored the cognitive activity involved in interacting with the various types of software. Two papers are of particular importance here, however. Gavriel Salomon (1990) discusses effects with and of the computer and Roy Pea (1985) talks of amplification versus the reorganisation of mental functions. Essentially they are both saying that we can use the computer either as a tyre lever to enhance our performance or we can enter into new ways of thinking. The survey evidence shows that good classrooms are using IT as a tool to enhance performance. Poor classrooms have not reached this stage at all. There is little evidence of teachers or students working beyond the performance enhancement stage. Indeed:

- Good current use of IT in classrooms is directed to performance enhancement.
- The use of computers as a reward rather than for enhancement is still with us.

The use of IT as a catalyst for change

There is an awareness that the use of IT should be investigated in context. An exciting development has been the coming together of two research agendas: investigations into co-operative and collaborative learning and the IT agenda (Light and Mavarech, 1992; Underwood, Underwood and Turner, 1993).The focus has moved from mental states to the social context of learning in which the computer can play many parts including that of 'significant other' in the Vygotskian sense. This awareness of the importance of the social context in teaching and learning leads full circle to Clark's criticism that you cannot separate the effect of the IT from other variables in the classroom. That may be so, but Gavriel Salomon in his paper 'The Flute vs. The Orchestra' argues why should you want to? If the computer brings about a change in social organisation that leads to educational benefits of some kind isn't that enough! On a down note Olson (1988) and many others have shown how resistant to change classroom settings are. It is in these classrooms we will see poor use of IT leading to few if any educational gains.

The National Curriculum context

Finally, whatever our own personal dreams for the education system may be, they have to be seen in terms of the National Curriculum. At the outset the government's strategy for IT in schools was to:

> 'harness the potential for IT for enhancing the quality of teaching and learning across the curriculum – whether in traditional technology or traditionally non-technology areas – and to extend that benefit as widely as possible. The familiarisation of pupils with new technology as an end in itself is intended as an important by-product of the programme, but not as a central focus.'

> (DES, 1989b, p.1)

The most significant point for me at the NCET's seminar 'Seen IT in the UK' held at the BETT 1994 was a remark from Philip Lewis in his short address on the Department for Education's (DFE) strategy for IT.

He was pointing out that the DFE wants IT in schools to reflect the use of IT in the 'real world' and with this end in mind DFE staff have been talking to domain experts. He gave the example of a mathematician who had informed the DFE that no real mathematics now goes on without the aid of IT and that IT was not only an essential tool of mathematicians but it was changing the very nature of mathematics itself!

I found Philip Lewis's positive response to this statement very uplifting. A confirmation of the earlier DES support for IT as a learning tool rather than an end in itself. Many of us have argued that IT can be more than a workhorse, it has the potential to change our patterns of thinking and our ways of knowing. My problem now, however, is to reconcile this new-found awareness of the power of IT with the National Curriculum and particular with the Dearing Report's focus on IT as a skill rather than as a cognitive tool. If I was one of the more traditional members of the DFE, or indeed of government, I would be horrified by the spectre raised by our unnamed mathematician's assertions of the power of IT. My policy would be to ban all machines immediately, because it is by emphasising the skills role of IT in the National Curriculum that its potential power as an agent for change is likely to drain away!

In this text all of the authors are looking at IT as a significant stimulus to children's thinking and learning. We make no apology for the fact that IT skills *per se* are a secondary consideration. In Chapters 2 and 10 the computer is a problem setter to which the children respond. Chapter 2 describes how variations in group composition influences the successful outcome of the task. The need for learners to respect and value each other's contribution to that task proves to be critical to the learning. Chapter 10 also looks at group problem solving but here the group includes both parents and children. Chapter 9 tackles the thorny problem of control technology in the classroom head-on by focusing on ways to enthuse girls, and indeed how to de-motivate them, through control technology. Chapters 3–8 look at key computer applications and the ways in which they can be constructively used to support cognitive, and in some cases, social development.

Chapter 2
Collaboration and problem solving: Gender differences and the quality of discussion

Geoffrey Underwood

When children work in groups there are benefits to be gained, but group work also carries risks. These risks are particularly high for certain combinations of children, computer role and task. It is this interaction between the social structure of the group, the computer as a possible 'other' person within the group, and the task in hand, which we will focus upon here. In doing so we are endeavouring to provide guidelines to successful learning outcomes through group work.

Boys, girls and computers are a dangerous combination. A mixed group around a computer can be characterised as boys arguing with each other about who controls the keyboard or the mouse, and girls as spectators. This is not because girls have any inherent disabilities or phobias about using computers (at least, not until after they have had unpleasant confrontations with a computer-bully), but because the boys see themselves as the rightful and superior users of the technology. Formal classroom observations have repeatedly reported girls sitting towards the back in computer classes, boys sitting with the right hand nearest the mouse, and girls being bullied away from control of the machine even though they express interest and then frustration at not being allowed to contribute (Culley, 1988; Barbieri and Light, 1992; Beynon, 1993).

These observations from classroom activities are reflected in the results from our controlled classroom experiments on the effectiveness of single gender and mixed gender pairs of children. In a series of studies we have used a Cloze task delivered with the INFANT TRAY program, in which a short passage of text has a number of letters replaced by hyphens. The task is to complete the passage by moving through the cursor and entering possible letters with the keyboard. Successful attempts result in the letter replacing the hyphen. An example of such a passage, as it first appears in one of our studies, is as follows[1:]

> THERE WAS ONCE A B-- C--L-D
> ETHELRED W-- W-- RE--Y F--
> A--T----. H- L-V-D I- A T---
> RI--- N-X- T- O-- O- T--S- B--
> JU----S F--L O- CR--OD---S,
> T-GE--, RUINED C----S A-- S--N-
> STATUES C-V--ED W--H V-N--.

With this task we have found that mixed gender (BG) pairs perform poorly in comparison with either boy–boy (BB) pairs or girl–girl (GG) pairs, using task performance measures such as the number of letters and words attempted in set time interval, and the number of letters and words that match those from the original passage. The mixed pairs in our first study (Underwood, McCaffrey and Underwood, 1990) performed less well than the single gender pairs, and it seemed to us, in informal observations, that the BGs were sharing the task in a different way to the BBs and the GGs. Whereas the BGs were alternating their use of the keyboard, the BBs and GGs were spending more time discussing the problem and thinking about the same part of the problem together.

This result is in contrast with Hughes and Greenhough's (1989) study of paired working with a programming task and a floor turtle. Their programming task found that GGs performed poorly in comparison with both the BBs and the BGs, whereas our Cloze task had the BGs performing least well. Hughes and Greenhough summarised their results as showing that whenever there was a boy present in a pair, then programming performance was good.

One resolution of this discrepancy that we have been able to suggest is in the ages of the children tested – Hughes and Greenhough observed very young primary school children while we worked with children towards the top of the primary age range. Alternatively, it could have been that the essentially linguistic nature of our task was critically different to the essentially spatial nature of the programming task. When we observed older children on a turtle task we did not find the

---

[1] In full: 'There was once a boy called Ethelred who was ready for anything. He lived in a town right next to one of those big jungles full of crocodiles, tigers, ruined cities and stone statues covered with vines.'

Hughes and Greenhough pattern of GGs at a disadvantage (Underwood, Underwood and Turner, 1993).

The task is certainly important, and different patterns of performance can be obtained by slight changes. Barbieri and Light (1992) had pairs of children work on a computer-based problem solving task presented in an adventure game format. The task required planning in order to move people (the King's servants: a driver, a ship's captain and an airman) around in various forms of transport (car, ship and plane) in order to transport the King's crown safely back to the King, avoiding pirates who block one of the direct routes. In view of the dispute between our results with the TRAY program (Underwood *et al.*, 1990) and Hughes and Greenhough's results with the floor turtle, the results were illuminating. The BBs outperformed the GGs, and the BGs were intermediate: a pattern similar to Hughes and Greenhough. The task is critical however, and the 'King's men vs. pirates' format is arguably more appealing to boys than to girls. This was confirmed in a similar study performed by Littleton *et al.* (1993). An isomorphic version of the 'King and Crown' was written, in which an identical planning task required the transport of various characters and an object between locations and avoiding an obstacle. In this case the characters were 'Honeybears', the object was a pot of honey, and the obstacle was Honeymonsters. The format was changed, but the task required an identical solution strategy.

The results changed dramatically, with GGs tending to outperform BBs with the Honeybears version of the problem, and BBs performing more effectively than the GGs with the King and Crown version. The boys were unaffected by task format, while the girls showed considerable sensitivity to the appearance of the problem. Karen Littleton and her colleagues attributed the effect to differences in 'levels of engagement' – the boys found the two formats to be equally appealing, but the girls were more motivated or more entertained by by the Honeybears version. The appearance of the task itself is important, and may be part of the explanation for the differences seen in different studies. Using our linguistic problem-solving task – the cloze task presented by the TRAY program – GGs are rarely outperformed, and BGs usually underperform. The problem now is to explain why boys and girls fail to work together effectively, and then to find ways of overcoming the problem.

The informal observation that the successful pairs of children were discussing the task with each other, and that this occurred principally with the single gender pairs, provided the question for our next study (Underwood, Jindal and Underwood, 1994). The successful performers discussed possible completions of the words and entertained each other's ideas, while the pairs who were eventually unsuccessful talked little to each other except to decide who was to have control of the keyboard. It is not talking itself that is related to success, because the subject of the discussion is important. In the study by Underwood *et al.* (1994) we presented essentially the same task to the same gender pairings, but actively encouraged some pairs to co-operate, to discuss the task, and to agree with each other before acting. The other pairs were told that their performance would be assessed individually, even though they would be working with a partner.

We followed up the informal observation that BB and GG pairs tended to talk about the problem and in particular about alternative ideas for the completion of words by formalising this relationship. All three combinations of children were observed, with half the pairs instructed explicitly that they should co-operate. They were told of the value of discussion, and that they should *agree* on any actions to be taken before any letters were to be attempted. The other pairs were told that their performance would be assessed on the basis of their *individual contribution*. The study therefore looked at the influence of collaboration, with BB, GG, and BG pairs, and asked whether our initial observation of poor performance with mixed pairs could be over-turned by getting them to work actively together. The instructions were effective, both in terms of the informal measures of discussion during performance and in terms of the enhanced success of co-operating pairs, except for the BGs. These pairs were generally poor performers, and the instructions had little effect upon them. The only effect was upon their general level of activity – the number of key presses made – but this was not reflected in the success with the task.

Instructions to collaborate also had a little effect upon the GGs, but this is not surprising given their generally high level of performance on the task. Regardless of instructions, the girls tended to work well together and to discuss the task. They clearly enjoyed collaborating, and the performance of any two girls was generally superior to that of any other pair. When given the non-collaboration instructions they still co-operated, and out-performed the BBs and the BGs. The girls worked as a team in any case, but when given collaboration instructions their performance also improved.

The performance of the BBs was interesting. When given instructions to work as individuals they performed poorly, at the level of the BGs, but when told to collaborate they did so, and then they performed at the level of the GGs. Instructions to collaborate had the greatest effect on the pairs of boys, and no effect on the mixed pairs. The BGs simply did not enjoy working together on this task.

A study reported by Fitzpatrick and Harding (1993) adds to this description of mixed gender pairs. Using a word completion task they again found that BBs and GGs co-operated in that they negotiated joint actions, relative to mixed pairs. The BGs worked asymmetrically, with one partner dominating, and usually the boy taking control of the keyboard. The single gender pairs also worked faster at the task. Howe, Tolmie and Anderson (1991) have also reported interaction failures for BGs in comparison with single gender pairs working with physics problems. Their BGs talked less, and problem solving success was related to specific characteristics of dialogue. The successful pairs tended to talk about possible explanatory factors and predictions in a problem concerning the paths taken by various falling objects.

What kinds of discussion between mixed and single gender pairs are associated with performance enhancement on the TRAY cloze task? We approached this question by recording the dialogue between children as they negotiated their way through the task (Underwood, Underwood and Turner, 1993). Each statement was categorised according to a Bales interaction analysis that breaks discussion into four main types: (1) group agreement, (2) offers suggestions/answers, (3) asks for suggestions/answers, and (4) group disagreement. We found several differences between the pairs using this analysis, and this is pointing towards an explanation of some of the performance differences. For example, and in this version of the task all pairs of children were told to collaborate, the GGs offered more suggestions than the other pairs, particularly offering more evaluation and analysis. The BGs offered negative socio-emotional comments more often than the other pairs, suggesting that they were disagreeing with each other more, and showing tension and antagonism. These results are in general agreement with other observations in the literature, with BGs tending to talk less about the task and with one partner dominant, especially with the boy partner taking control of the keyboard/mouse (Barbieri and Light, 1992; Fitzpatrick and Harding, 1993).

It would be premature to conclude that mixed gender pairs cannot work together, and many teachers have personal experiences of BGs working well in their classrooms. All pairings *can* work well, but on the whole BGs tend to work less well. What we need to know about are the circumstances surrounding effective working. There may be specific tasks that can be used to encourage effective co-operation – we have reviewed some interactions between gender and tasks here – and successful performance may be predicted by discussions taking certain courses. There are some hints about the association between certain kinds of discussion and successful performance in the classroom studies described above, and before looking at the nature of dialogue in detail, consider a discussion between a highly successful pair of 11 year olds. Although BGs tend not to work well together their performance is exceptional in a number of ways.

What follows is part of a transcript of the discussion between Laura and Steven as they work through a short passage in a TRAY task. At this point they have been working for a few minutes, and the task is half completed. The passage is the section of text in the 'Ethelred' example presented earlier. The transcript is taken from a study conducted with Karen Pheasey, in which pairs of 10- and 11-year-old children work to complete the letters and words of a short passage. The interesting features of this particular section of transcript all concern the extent of the co-operation between Laura and Steven. Although they have, on the whole, shared the keyboard (Steven chose to sit on the right, and therefore has control of the cursor keys, and Laura takes the keyboard letters), they are solving the problems in the passage co-operatively. They address the same problem words, they each make suggestions about candidate letters and words, they act upon each other's suggestions and they evaluate each other's ideas.

75. Steven	THERE ONCE WAS A BOY CALLED ETHELRED WHO WAS READY FOR ANYTHING ... HE LIVED IN TOWN RIGHT NEXT TO ONE OF ... it's got to be OF
76. Laura	we tried O [*Laura* types F]
77. Steven	oh! obviously we didn't
78. Laura	no I pressed delete [*Steven* moves cursor]
79. Steven	OF ... NEXT TO ONE OF THOSE
80. Laura	yeah [*Laura* types H O E]
81. Steven	S
82. Laura	NEXT TO ONE OF THOSE BIG ... I know, CROCODILES [*Steven* moves cursor]
83. Steven	naaah
84. Laura	no, go on let's try it, go on [*Laura* types O C I L E]
85. Steven	CROC-O-DILES yes! I've got it right
86 Laura	ON NEXT TO ... right THERE ONCE WAS A BOY CALLED ETHELRED WHO WAS READY FOR ANYTHING
87. Steven	no THERE ONCE WAS A BOY CALLED ETHELRED [disputes pronunciation of ETHELRED – he prefers "E-THE-L-RED"]
88. Laura	HE LIVED IN A TOWN RIGHT NEXT TO ONE OF THOSE BIG something something
89. Steven	try that [*Laura* types F] OF CROCODILES [*Steven* moves cursor]

90. Laura	yeah erm A BIG FULL FULL FULL [*Laura* types U L]
91. Steven	FULL OF BIG [*Steven* moves cursor]
92. Laura	BIG
93. Laura	It's something like a river or something like that
94. Steven	pardon?
95. Laura	A BIG something FULL OF CROCODILES
96. Steven	JUNGLES
97. Laura	yeah JUNGLES let's try it [*Laura* types N G L E]
98. Steven	ONE OF THOSE BIG JUNGLES [*Steven* moves cursor]
99. Laura	yeah
100. Steven	told you
101. Laura	oh yeah
102. Both (together)	TIGERS [*Steven* moves cursor] [*Laura* types I G]
103. Steven	TIGE
104. Laura	delete it [*Laura* types E R S] E R S [*Steven* moves cursor] RUINED TIGERS RUINED CARVED no CAVED no WASH [*Laura* types A S]
105. Steven	[*Steven* moves cursor] WITH no [*Laura* types I T] [*Steven* moves cursor]
106. Laura	oh yes sorry I did it wrong ... WITH oh let's try this one right THERE ONCE WAS A BOY CALLED ETHELRED
107. Steven	E-THE-L-RED [disputing pronunciation again]
108. Laura	E-THE-L-RED WHO WAS READY FOR ANYTHING ... HE LIVED IN A TOWN RIGHT NEXT TO ONE OF THOSE BIG JUNGLES FULL OF CROCODILES TIGERS RUINED
109. Steven	CAVES
110. Laura	CAVES no it can't be
111. Steven	try it
112. Laura	no it can't be [*Laura* types a V] look
113. Steven	put E [*Laura* types E]
114. Laura	CITIES
115. Steven	never
116. Laura	go on, just try that [*Laura* types I T E] CIT-IES [*Laura* types I presses return] I
117. Steven	CITIES
118. Laura	AND [*Laura* types N D]

(Task continues to completion of the passage, with 142 statements.)

Each of the children in the transcript presented here is comfortable making suggestions about possible entries. In lines 82, 104, 114 and

118, for instance, it is Laura who is suggesting the words, and Steven makes suggestions in lines 75, 79, 96, 109 and elsewhere. In line 102 they suggest a solution at the same time. These suggestions are often challenged – Steven in line 103, incorrectly, and Laura in line 110, correctly – but the important point is that suggestions are not ignored. They are evaluated. Consider Laura's correct challenge in line 110, for example, followed by persistence from Steven (line 111), and in line 112 Laura tries the suggested word and demonstrates that it does not work. This is hypothesis testing, and the discussion traces the course of the children's thinking. A further encouraging feature of this pair of thinkers is that they are using the meaning of the whole text in making suggestions about the words to be discovered. It is not possible to say, of course, whether this intelligent approach to the problem would have been observed in the absence of discussion. We cannot say whether the discussion is merely an artefact of the children's thinking – a record of what was going through their minds – or whether it has acted as a catalyst to help them to work through the problem. What we can say is that these two partners can be seen to be working towards the same goal and to be sharing their thoughts about alternative hypotheses. Something similar can be seen in the Maple Leaf transcript (Underwood and Underwood, 1990) with a mixed group of primary school children working with database questions. This idea that cognitive progress is made through the evaluation of alternative hypotheses is something that is worth exploring, and it can be reconsidered with a description of some non-CBL tasks reported recently. They will be reviewed shortly.

There is clearly a sense of group cohesion and group responsibility between Laura and Steven: they value each others' inputs and have developed a group etiquette. There is no sign of the negative comments or destructive criticisms which lead to tension and antagonism in our study of the TRAY mixed gender pairings. Not that all pairs work this well: another mixed gender pair made very few comments at all, communicating by occasionally grunting at each other. Indeed, we were so surprised about how quiet they were that we wondered whether the microphone had ceased operating. With the volume turned up to maximum we could hear very clearly the children in the corridor outside the test room, and we could hear the keys clicking as the members of the pair took turns to move the cursor and to enter letters, but there was no verbal communication. Their style was turn-taking, with little indication of collaboration.

The recurring observation from natural classroom tasks is that boys see the computer as being in their domain, but classroom experiments find that in single gender groups the GGs perform at least as well as the

BBs. It is only when paired boys and girls are paired together that they perform poorly. Ann Cale Kruger's (1993) analysis of collaborative styles helps us to understand the dynamics of paired interactions and their effects upon thinking skills. Her studies of paired reasoning with socio-moral problems showed that the nature of the discussion influenced subsequent performance. Pairs that offered suggestions to a problem, and considered each other's suggestions, did better in an individual test of reasoning administered later. In particular, it was the consideration of rejected solutions that was associated with the development of thinking. Kruger related this finding to the Piagetian/ Vygotskian debate about conflict and co-operation, suggesting that if conflict means a discussion about explanations and questions, and if co-operation means an agreement with a clarification and a development or explanation, then there isn't much to choose between them. In operational terms conflict then starts to resemble co-operation and the debate loses its focus, but what is really important is that cognitive development will proceed through the consideration of alternative solutions to a problem, and this is where discussion can help.

Kruger (1993) has recently reviewed the evidence that suggests that when pairs of children solve a problem together, they think more effectively than when they work alone. This generalisation is good for a variety of tasks, including Piagetian conservation, logical thinking, moral reasoning, and mathematics. Different theoretical perspectives on this advantage give different explanations of course, but Kruger's compromise explanation points to the similarities between them. This conclusion also comes from Azmitia and Montgomery's (1993) investigation of logical reasoning. Pairs of 11-year-old children discussed problems involving associations between variables, and the pairs solving the greatest number of problems also engaged in dialogues in which they evaluated possible solutions and justified their proposals. They considered alternative suggestions. The 'conflict' inherent in the proposal and discussion of contradictory hypotheses is equivalent to the mutual consideration of each other's ideas.

Discussion provides the opportunity to compare ideas, and to evaluate suggestions, something that the GG pairs in our TRAY cloze tasks were doing with little encouragement from us. In the case of the BG pairs there was been little discussion and generally unimpressive performance. The transcript from Laura and Steven provides a notable exception to this pattern. The most effective thinkers justify their own ideas and also take account of their partner's suggestions, with the eventual rejection of failed solutions being the best indicator of new understanding. Now that we know what current patterns of performance look like, and how children tend to discuss problems when working around a computer, we can encourage the kind of discussion that will result in the development of their powers of thinking. When we have observed mixed pairs working successfully together each child has been comfortable in offering suggestions and in analysing and evaluating each other's suggestions, as can be seen in the dialogue between Laura and Steven.

Recent studies of the benefits of group work have emphasised the Piagetian idea of socio-cognitive conflict resulting in decentralised thinking or the Vygotskian perspective by which social co-operation delivers new cognitive products. Conflicts can certainly be observed when mixed gender groups work with computers, but they are generally associated with impoverished performance. Single gender pairs tend to work most effectively, and analyses of the on-task discussions point to a relationship between analytic and evaluative comments and successful performance. These comments tend to be missing in the discussions between boys and girls.

The nature of the co-operation between the participants may differ within and between these learning environments. Currently terms such as group work, co-operative and collaborative learning are used very loosely in the literature. The central concept refers to learning environments in which small groups of students work together to achieve a common goal. In achieving that common goal, however, the members of the group may choose to take responsibility for sub-tasks and work co-operatively, or they may collaborate and work together on all parts of the problem. If the learners collaborate and share in the decision-making process the level of social interaction is necessarily high, but this is not necessarily so for co-operative workers.

There are essential differences in the level of interaction in co-operative versus collaborative work group, so how might these affect learning? There is a myriad of questions still to be answered in this area. What do children gain from social interaction and under what circumstances do those gains occur? What aspects of children's social interaction contribute to children's advances? How do variations in the nature of the group – such as whether the partners are adults or peers, the extent of their expertise, their authority or equality relative to the learner, and the extent to which partners share in decision making – affect the nature of the interaction and therefore the learning that takes place? Are there any differences in the role of the interaction depending on the age of the children? Essentially we have been considering the circumstances under which children's thinking can gain from co-operative problem-solving with computer-based activities, and the causes of these gains.

The Piagetian perspective argues that gains are made through socio-cognitive conflict, which acts against ego-centric thought. By coming up against the ideas of a co-worker children see a challenge to their own interpretation of the world. This social conflict requires a cognitive resolution, and so cognitive gains are made. On the other hand, the explanation from Vygotsky's perspective is that social co-operation results in a new cognitive product based upon joint definitions. Whereas the Piagetian perspective sees conflict as the key, the Vygotskian approach is to emphasise the value of co-operation. Kruger's resolution is through an analysis of the interactions between children attempting to solve problems together, and her account provides us with an explanation of why some groups of children working on a computer task perform better than others, as well as giving some hints about how the effective classroom will be organised.

Kruger's resolution sees conflict as resembling co-operation when it makes us understand a problem from another perspective and when alternative solutions are entertained. The case study of Laura and Steven presented in this chapter provides an example of productive co-operation with the appearance of conflict. Suggestions are made by each partner, and are challenged. Each partner's ideas are evaluated. Their hypotheses are tested, and the eventual outcome is a totally successful exercise, both in terms of the solution of the problem and in terms of their enjoyment in thinking about written language. The transcript illustrates productive discussions between children in a mixed gender pair, in contrast with the failures of co-operation reported in some of our earlier reports. Laura and Steven's case study provides a notable exception to this pattern, and indicates the type of discussion to be fostered if a successful collaboration is to be seen in the computer classroom.

Chapter 3
Word processing and desk-top publishing

Brent Robinson
with Pam Bloomfield and Jane Carson

Word-processing and desk top-publishing packages are by far the most common applications of information technology (IT) used in schools. According to HMI (1992, p.3) more than one third of all lessons involving IT which were observed between 1988 and 1992 made use of these packages. Why should this be the case?

To understand the popularity of these packages, it is important to consider carefully the nature of the software. Word-processing and desk-top publishing programs are concerned essentially with the manipulation of information – textual and graphic. They allow users to process information and this is an activity which at the heart of learning. From the earliest days of the National Curriculum, this fact was acknowledged. The first report from the expert group devising what should be taught in English noted that:

> 'Education deals centrally with information... so the development of a tech-
> nology designed precisely to store, sort, search and transmit huge amounts
> of information at high speed is potentially of great relevance to [teachers]
> and their pupils'

> (DES, 1988, para. 14.16 & 14.17)

Word-processing programs allow the user to input, edit, correct and present texts of any kind. While they differ widely in the facilities they offer writers all but the very crudest offer opportunities for text insertion, substitution and rearrangement. Sophisticated word-processing programs offer considerable control over the final presentation of a text: a variety of typefaces can be used; text can be blocked or printed in columns and even graphic images can be inserted in the document. Desk-top publishing programs provide further control over the composition and presentation of finished documents. Writers sometimes compose text with a word processor and then import it into a desk-top publishing program to enhance the text's presentation. Here, further attention can be given to the style of typeface and its size, the placing of the text on the page and the incorporation of other features like frames around blocks of print and visual icons to break up the text. Graphics can also be incorporated into a desk-top published document. These may be original images created in a design package and then imported into the desk-top program. Images can also be captured from other printed material using a scanner, or from a moving video source using a digitiser, and pasted into the document. Recent desk-top publishing packages allow users to build both text and images simultaneously, typing directly into the document alongside positioned images. Indeed, modern desk-top publishing packages incorporate powerful text-processing features, making the prior use of a word processor redundant. As word processors themselves also increasingly include graphic features, it is becoming increasingly hard to distinguish between word-processing and desk-top publishing software.

There are many occasions when such a powerful resource can be used in the curriculum. Written language serves many purposes within learning. It is used by students in school to record ideas and to communicate meaning to others. Increasingly, teachers are also recognising that writing has cognitive functions for the student in clarifying and supporting thought – conceiving and recollecting ideas, organising them, reconstructing them, reviewing and hypothesising (DES, 1989a, para. 17.46). Typically, these purposes are seen in the form of a continuum, one in which it is increasingly recognised that the computer has a role to play:

- drafting (getting ideas on to paper or computer screen, regardless of form, organisation or expression);
- redrafting (shaping and structuring the raw material – either on paper or screen – to take account of purpose, audience and form);
- rereading and revising (making alterations that will help the reader);
- proof reading.

(DES, 1989a, para. 17.48).

These stages are not necessarily discrete nor are they strictly linear. Writing can very often be a recursive process as writers redraft their work (Emig, 1982). Sophisticated writers also frequently attempt all the stages simultaneously, writing only a single and final copy of their work. But using a computer to support writing activities enables writers to tease apart these stages of the writing process, separating in particular composition (the cognitive stages of the writing process) from final public communication. Optimum use of word-processing and desk-top publishing packages depends upon an appropriate match of the writing activity with the facilities of the electronic medium.

Computers and the cognitive functions of writing

Frank Smith (NATE, 1991) separates the task of writing into two broad aspects: composition and transcription. Composition is concerned with the development of ideas while transcription is concerned with the surface features of language. Smith argues that normally 'composition and transcription interfere with each other' (para. 1.2). When composing text on paper, writers have to concern themselves simultaneously with choosing, editing, formatting and printing words. The mechanics of production are apt to interfere with the process of creation. By contrast, when using a computer, writers may keep distinct the stages of composition and production. So if writers do not have to concern themselves with the ultimate style and presentation of their work at the outset, they can concentrate far more on the ideas themselves.

It is important to realise that writing and thinking are closely entwined. Schutz (1982) has characterised writing as 'catching the world of inner experience in the net of language' (p.130). Vygotsky (1978) claims that by verbalising our ideas, we are required not only to articulate them but also cognitively to restructure them. Clark (1984) argues that we write before and while we think, while Freedman and Pringle (1989) state that new meanings are made through the active and continued involvement of the writer with the unfolding text.

If writing and thinking are so closely related, how can we use computers to facilitate the composition of our thoughts? Stephen Marcus (Marcus and Blau, 1983) suggests that when students are engaged in the early stages of composition at a computer, brainstorming and getting down their first ideas, teachers might turn off the screen so that students cannot see what they are typing at the keyboard. Initially students might be disorientated, but the technique shows dramatically that users do not have to attend to all the stages of the writing process at once:

'The absence of visual feedback from the text they were producing actually sharpened their concentration on each of the writing tasks, enhanced their fluency, and yielded texts that were more, rather than less, cohesive. The invisible writing procedure seemed to force the participants to give more concentrated and sustained attention to their emerging thoughts than they ordinarily gave when composing with a working pen or pencil. Some students reported that when they wrote under ordinary conditions they would usually allow their minds to wander after each sentence or pair of sentences. Rarely did they keep their attention focused undeviatingly on a single train of thought for more than one or two sentences. In addition, students noted that their usual pattern in composing was to interrupt the flow of their thought frequently to edit and amend the language, syntax or mechanics of their developing text. The experiment suggested to them that their usual pauses obstruct their fluency and, more importantly, dilute their concentration. Under the conditions of the experiment they could neither edit, nor rewrite, nor allow their attention to stray from the line of thought they were developing.' (p.12)

Of course, once the ideas are committed to the computer, then the machine is unique in its ability to move text around allowing users to regroup their ideas, forming new associations, categorisations and logical developments. Edward de Bono (1983) suggested far more use could be made of the screen in the early stages of composition. According to de Bono, the very name 'word processor' limits a user's vision: 'You'd get a lot more out of our machines if you called them "thought processors" and used them for solving problems'. As an example, he suggests making use of multiple windows on screen, each being used for word processing. First of all, the user brainstorms about a topic, typing into a single window every random thought which comes to mind. This list is then refined: the text is scrolled through the window and ideas are moved across to a second window where they are grouped in categories or ordered in a logical sequence.

Alternatively, there might be several windows open, each one being used to store a different category of idea. In this way, the computer can help writers to structure and record their thoughts. The aim might be ultimately to synthesise the various groups of ideas into a coherent linear text. On the other hand, modern desk-top publishing allows the presentation of several texts together on the screen and printout. It is important too to remember that some ideas are best presented graphically rather than linguistically and that some computer users will find that they can work conceptually and communicate better with pictures and images instead of, or alongside, text. Desk-top publishing offers users this potential.

It seems that hypertext and multimedia software will increase again the possibilities. This software is the subject of another chapter in this book but it is worth noting here that such software provides a variety of tools to explore and communicate ideas. The role of hypertext could be to:

'...act as a repository for all sorts and sizes of pieces of text, graphics or whatever on a subject of interest. New items would be linked to others as they were added, on the basis of whatever intuitive connections or associations the writer senses might exist. Such links would be subsequently deleted, added to or moved as the writer's thinking evolved, and a clearer conception of the subject emerged. The structure of the developing hypertext would thus model the author's current pattern of thinking about the subject, and would be likely to lead to a network with many links rather than few, and with no obvious hierarchical structure. This approach fits well with a view of writing as an intensely personal activity, in which the aim is to crystallise and express the writer's viewpoint as authentically as possible, without imposing unnecessary external constraints.'

(Scrimshaw, 1993, p.175)

Unfortunately, the potential educational benefits of word processing and desk-top publishing (let alone hypermedia) do not appear to have been as fully realised in composition as in transcription. Daiute (1986) in the USA and Trushell (1986) in the UK found that while students appeared to edit more with a word processor than on paper, they made fewer structural changes to their ideas. Instead, attention was paid to spelling, punctuation and grammar, all of which improved markedly when using a word processor. Later studies have tended to confirm these findings. Comments like this are typical:

'I was hoping for dramatic changes of the kind we see in writers' notebooks – and more use of clauses, or complex sentences – with children wanting to use the more powerful word processing commands; few of these types of change were made.'

(NATE, 1991, para 1.8.2)

To understand this we must take a number of factors into account. In the first place of course, we must consider carefully what features are actually provided by the software we offer young writers. Surprisingly, some of the word processors specifically aimed at schools have not contained even an elementary facility for the block moving of text, and where such features are present, they can still be irritating to use. We must not forget too, as Pullinger and Wellavize (1984) pointed out, trying to read and edit a text on screen is rather like trying to read a newspaper through a peephole in a piece of card. Pullinger and Wellavize found that students had problems in locating information and reading their texts critically. Fortunately, the advent of a windows environment on modern computers has gone a long way to allow users to see separate sections of the same text or different drafts of a text simultaneously while the cut and paste facility allows easy restructuring of ideas. Even so, it is interesting to note that '...many teachers have independently come to the conclusion that it is better for students to review their texts away from the computer' (Potter, 1988a, p.5).

The computer's capacity to rearrange texts easily does not, by itself, encourage students to revise. Daiute (1986) suggests two further factors to take into account. It could be argued that complex text manipulation comes with greater maturity and with the ability to move from the concrete to the abstract, something which only develops as pupils grow older. This ties in with the Piagetian concept that a child's development of language and perceptual abilities is not simply a miniature of an adult's: the process of changes in a child's writing must not be compared with those of an adult (Piaget, 1982; Nelson, undated).

The second point made by Daiute – and more recently reiterated by Cochrane-Smith (1991) in her extensive review of the research – is that writers need to have text manipulation demonstrated and must practise it themselves as young writers (rather than as computer operators) to make use of the facilities afforded by word processors. After all, for many students in school the majority of their writing is still conducted away from a computer in a conceptual world firmly rooted in the idea of writing as manuscript (Peacock, 1987).

As Papert (1980) has argued, the computer is a protean machine: its strength and its weakness lie in its versatility. While word processing and desk-top publishing offer many features to enable writers to manipulate text and images, exactly how users do so once they are shown them is up to them. Unless writers understand the nature of the different stages of the writing process, they will not appreciate fully the value of the technical facilities available to them. They can become fixated on the more obvious facilities of the medium, the ones related to those aspects of writing they have always been taught to be concerned with. In one case study (NATE, 1991) a teacher of Key Stage 1 pupils noted that they were 'excited by the pleasure they got from seeing their ideas appear immediately in print on the screen' but they were also 'quick to spot any mistakes I [the teacher] made typing out their ideas and wanted to make immediate corrections'; while a teacher working with a range of Key Stage 3 and 4 students noted that they were all 'very concerned with the appearance of the text.... Corrections were made as they discovered, not left until the end' (para. 1.8.2). As computers become more sophisticated, the ability to create attractive, near-professional final results prompts writers from the outset to pay even more attention to the surface linguistic and presentational features of what they write at the expense of other aspects of composition. Fanatical font fiddling becomes more important than the ideas the writer is actually wrestling to articulate.

The role of the teacher seems crucial in helping young writers to appreciate and attend to all the stages of the writing process not just the transcriptional aspects and to use the computer effectively at each stage. As Graves has argued (1982), students cannot develop their writing skills unless they learn to revise and redraft their work. Now with the advent of the computer he pointedly remarks 'I think marvellous things can be done with the computer as word processor – if it's in the hands of someone who really knows writing' (Green, 1984). To take an extreme but not uncommon example, there are teachers who allow students to use a word processor just to type up an already hand drafted and corrected text so that it can be attractively printed for display purposes. The activity is really nothing more than copy typing for the sake of the final audience.

Even where pupils do work through the early stages of composition on a computer, it is frequently with the final aim of producing a text for a wider audience. The role of the technology as a means of helping students to apprehend and process ideas exclusively for themselves has not yet been widely developed or adopted in schools. Not all writing activities on the computer should inevitably end in an advanced presentational form: 'Not every writing activity will demand a focus upon audience, nor an awareness of the relation between form and content' (NATE, 1991, para. 1.27). The text and image processing features of the software can be used to help the students make sense of ideas for themselves rather than for others. Teachers, in negotiation with children, should make conscious decisions about which programs will assist the learning which takes place and how best to use them.

Computers, writing and communication

According to Vygotsky (1978), our patterns of communication and interaction with others highly influence the ways in which we organise and interpret information. Other researchers concentrate on the conflicts which may develop during an interaction: 'It is the construction of meanings by the speaker, their reconstructions by the listener and the contradiction that can arise in the process which can generate increased understanding' (Balacheff and Laborde, 1984, p. 4). Because of the public nature of the screen, the computer quite naturally becomes a focus for interaction and collaboration among writers and its value in this respect has been emphasised many times (e.g. Baskerville, 1986; Somekh, 1986; Trushell, 1986). Gallagher (1985) claims that the special characteristics of word processing make it an instrument that 'lends itself, both psychologically and materially' to the practice of collaborative learning 'and not just in the writing class, but in any class where students are required to write' (p.4). Similarly, Sudol (1985) states that the use of word processing offers an opportunity to 'reinvent' the workshop classroom model in which collaborative learning takes place and where the students are liberated from the idea that what they write is 'for teachers to evaluate'.

Because of the particular nature of the medium, the role of the teacher can change radically, becoming that of active participant in the writing process.

> 'The most remarkable feature of this [word processing] program is that it has given me an opportunity which I had previously missed: to sit with a group of children and make an in-depth study of their creative writing, and discuss with them the changes they could make to improve it.'
>
> (NATE, 1991, para. 1.2)

Nancy Martin (1976) has argued that the teacher should in any case become someone to be communicated with rather than an assessor. Across the curriculum the teacher should engage in dialogue with students as they attempt to construct meaning in their writing. Seen from a Vygotskian perspective, there is a strong argument (Scrimshaw, 1993) that the teacher 'must be seen as an active communicative participant in learning, with the computer acting as a medium that creates new possibilities for learning and communication between teachers and learners' (p.5).

While both the public screen and the 'publication' afforded by printout offer potential for collaboration, they also seem to encourage a keen sense of audience. (Indeed, the collaborators themselves are, in one sense, an audience too.) In reviewing the early literature on the subject, Potter (1988b) noted that the large screen display '...can emphasise the public communicative nature of writing to the children – and develop their sense of audience'. He also noted that 'another very important feature is the printout, as this naturally leads to the publication of children's writing, which again emphasises the public communicative nature of writing, and develops a sense of audience' (p.6). Earl (1987) and Malone (1987) both regarded this as an essential element of the use of the word processor.

As part of any literacy programme in schools, students should of course develop the ability they will need as adults to write appropriately for several different audiences. But there are also immediate educational benefits wherever in the curriculum students are given an opportunity to write for authentic audiences. In drafting material to suit a particular audience, students will need to have mastery of the content and appreciate the ways in which readers will want, or need, to approach the material. This will involve cognitive restructuring and articulating of the material and this is likely to improve the writer's own understanding of it. The sense of audience for students' writing also appears to heighten motivation and a willingness to engage with the subject in question:

> 'The encouragement to write was most noticeable when the children were writing to produce a book or a newspaper. They seemed to be highly motivated and achieved success; their work was integrated with the topic and they were writing for a purpose. It seemed to be that they knew the work would be read by other people and so the task of writing became more real.'
>
> (Brent Micro-Technology Education Centre, 1988, p.12)

Computers, communication and the National Curriculum

From its inception, the National Curriculum has been a curriculum which acknowledges both the cognitive and communicative roles of language within it.

> '[Pupils] should learn to use writing to facilitate their own thinking and learning, recognising that not all written work will lead to a polished, final product. They should be able to record their first thoughts, capture immediate responses and collect and organise ideas so that they are available for reflection.... Pupils should have opportunities to write for a range of communicative or informative purposes including describing, explaining, giving instructions, reporting, expressing a point of view.... Pupils should learn how to organise and express their meaning appropriately for different specified audiences.
>
> (DES, 1989a, para. 17.48)

Within English this is self-evident but the importance of communication appears in less obvious contexts. The programme of study for Science, for example, stresses that the abilities to communicate, to apply, to investigate and to use scientific and technological knowledge and ideas to make informed judgements are essential elements in the study of science (DES, 1991, Programme of Study, Key Stage 4). The process should begin from Key Stage 1 where: 'Through their study of science, children should develop and use communication skills and techniques involved in obtaining, presenting and responding to information'. By Key Stage 4, pupils 'should be encouraged to articulate their own ideas ... they should have the opportunity to translate information from one form to another to suit audience and purpose...'. In Technology too, there is an emphasis on the importance of communicative abilities among pupils. The 1990 Technology Order stated that pupils should be able to develop, communicate and act upon an evaluation of the processes, products and effects of their design and technological activities; by Key Stage 4 pupils should certainly 'present their proposals to

an audience, using a range of methods and media' (DES, 1990).
Taking the National Curriculum as a whole, it is essentially what may
be termed a communicative curriculum in which: 'pupils should come
to develop a positive view of themselves as writers who are capable of
making and receiving meaning using a variety of forms depending on
audience and purpose' (DES, 1989a, para. 17.14). Within such a
curriculum, the computer as a communication device finds a ready
home. It is not surprising that the Technology working group considering the curricular role of information technology seized upon the
potential of the computer as a communication device, requiring that
'Pupils should be able to use IT appropriately and effectively to
communicate and handle information in a variety of forms and for a
variety of purposes...' (DES, 1989b, Attainment Target 5). The resulting
order required pupils to 'use information technology to retrieve,
develop, organise and present work' (Level 4) and to 'select software
and use it to produce reports which combine different forms of information to fulfil specific purposes for a variety of audiences' (Level 7).

Across the National Curriculum documents, computers therefore
often occur wherever communication is discussed. Modern Languages,
like English, provides a context for the use of word-processing and
desk-top publishing and the curriculum suggests that in learning and
using the target language, pupils should have regular opportunities to
use computers for drafting and redrafting, desk-top publishing and
communicating via electronic mail. In the humanities too, as suggested
in History, pupils should have opportunities to present meanings orally,
visually and in writing, using a range of techniques including
computers. And in Science, the emphasis on communication already
discussed has naturally implicated the computer: 'Pupils should use
computers to store, retrieve and present their work and extend their
understanding of information transfer' (DES, 1991, Programme of
Study, Key Stage 2).

The case studies

The case studies which follow reveal teachers trying to put into practice
within the curriculum some of the ideas discussed in this chapter. At
first sight, the case studies do not demonstrate the very high quality of
printed product which students can now obtain with the technology.
That takes a considerable investment of time and money. Rather, these
case studies show what can be achieved in the average school given the
limited time and typical resources which might be available. The
printed logos in the second activity in Case Study 1 and the newspaper

front page in Case Study 2 are typical of what might be achieved in many classrooms. But as this chapter has argued, the *process* of writing with a computer is as valuable educationally as is the final *product* and this dynamic, interactive process is more difficult to capture. Even so, the case studies do reveal teachers attending to the process of writing and using the technology to support it.

Case Study 1 includes two activities clearly showing how one teacher was thinking carefully about the nature of the computer medium and how best to suit it to the different aspects of the writing process. In the first activity, the teacher was keen to use the computer to assist in the early stages of composition. She developed a highly structured activity to stimulate the creation of ideas – what she calls a 'flow of consciousness' technique. Working under pressure of time, the students were asked to load into the computer a succession of files to which they had to respond in writing. The prepared files themselves had been written by the teacher in a syntactically loose note form and this encouraged the pupils to write in the same style themselves. The time constraint also prompted them to brainstorm and write notes rather than continuous prose. It was only when this stage of the writing process was complete that the students were subsequently brought back to the computer to revise their ideas and attend to the presentational features of their writing.

The second activity in this case study shows the same teacher using the computer appropriately for a writing activity which is right at the public, communicative end of the writing spectrum. On this occasion it was entirely appropriate to encourage the students from the outset to make use of the advanced presentational opportunities of the medium. The class was studying Shakespeare's *Julius Caesar* and the task was to design a logo for the political party represented by Brutus. Because of time constraints, the activity had to begin away from the computer. This is an activity in which the sense of audience is present right from the start and the computer is used to explore how best to achieve effective visual communication.

The second case study again demonstrates a teacher thinking carefully how to harness the technology appropriately and effectively for student's writing. The first activity was set with a clear sense of purpose and audience: the students were to write an estate agent's description of their school. The teacher was careful, however, to divide the writing activity into clearly defined stages. First, the students made notes away from the computer. Then they entered them on the machine with the teacher realising the need to intervene to show them how to use the manipulative features of the technology to arrange their ideas. The students were prompted to experiment on screen with the particular style of writing required, making use of the computer thesaurus when redrafting their work. Finally, once spelling, grammar and punctuation were corrected and the use of colour and type style carefully considered, the pupils added a title and printed out their work.

The final activity in the case study shows a more advanced presentational activity. The students had already undertaken a project on rivers and pollution but were subsequently asked to present their findings as a newspaper. The study shows how the students reworked their material in a variety of ways helping them, through the activity of writing, to understand their subject more fully and to generate new meanings for themselves.

The case studies further testify to some of the other well-documented advantages of the use of word-processing and desk-top publishing packages in schools. This chapter has concentrated on their use to develop facility in writing and to promote understanding. But these packages also motivate students, encourage collaboration and social interaction and offer greater parity of access to the curriculum (National Writing Project, 1990). Word-processing and desk-top publishing are thus powerful educational tools and it is not inappropriate that their use, according to the recent HMI survey noted at the beginning of this chapter, is becoming widespread in the curriculum. HMI believe that: 'the benefit of using IT to frame, develop and present ideas in writing is widely accepted by teachers' (HMI, 1992, p.2). The benefits can be seen across the whole curriculum in terms of motivation and interaction but they become particularly significant in those contexts in all subjects where writing is used to help students' cognitive and communicative development.

Case Study 1:

Creative Writing – 'Kidnapped!'
&
Designing a Political Poster
Pam Bloomfield
Leader of Language, Literature and Communication
Westfield School, Watford, Herts

Aims and Objectives
Activity 1: Creative Writing – 'Kidnapped!'
The aim was to create a structured story within a 'simulated' environment using 'flow of consciousness' style and to encourage development from the drafting stage using IT.

The Class
30 year-9 mixed-ability girls; 70% of them were Asian

Software	**Hardware**
FlexiWrite	15 RM Nimbus net

Project Description

Organisation

The class was divided into pairs to start with because there were not enough machines for one each but this also added to the fun of creating a story. I led the simulation by suggesting the background to what was happening to them in the fiction. Then at my command they would load up each pre-made file in turn (Figure 3.1) and add their immediate thoughts and feelings about the situation. There were very strict time allocations on this first draft because we had to get through all seven files in one hour. Pairs took it in turn to write down ideas.

Figure 3.1 Kidnapped simulation exercise – these are separate files brought in at various stages of the story setting

---

K1 Special day, no one cares! Trouble at home, trouble at school – terrible day. Kept back at the end of the day. Everyone has gone home. All alone. Dark. Raining. Cold.

K2 Two strangers in car. Expensive looking car. Stops. Walk on. One person gets out. Lift home ? No. Walk on. Paper bag on head. Hands tied. Thrown in car. It drives off.

K3 Back seat, sprawled out. Hands behind back. Thrown about as car turns comers. Where to ? Can't see. Can hear. "Have we got the right one ?" Right one what ? Is this a joke ? Help !

Next lesson, the files were separated so each individual could redraft their own version (Figure 3.2).

Outcomes

The pupils shared the experience of story writing; they learned how to put thoughts down on screen in rough form, the structure of a story and how to upgrade drafts to a finished product. The end result was enthusiasm!

The pupils were motivated primarily by the subject but also by the style of learning and novelty and lastly the software.

Figure 3.2 The Individual Stories

VICTIMS OF PLEASURE

It's my birthday today and nobody cares I'm 13!!! Trouble at home, my brother had to leave home today! Trouble at school – terrible day. Kept back at the end of the day for some stupid reason that I wore a badge!! Everyone has gone home, I'm all alone, it's getting dark. It's bloody RAINING and it is so bloody COLD.

If I was dead no one would notice where I was then either. I bet nobody is too bothered about where I am. Nobody wants me, does it come as any surprise?

Two strangers in a car, what are they looking at? Still it is an expensive looking car it's stopped. Who cares? I'm not going to turn around I'll just walk on. One person gets out.
  "Lift home?"
  NO!! GET LOST EVERYONE!!!
Who has put this paper bag on my head? Oh no my hands are tied. What are they doing? Who do they think they are throwing me in the car like that? We're moving, where are we going? It drives off.

Typical it had to happen to me, I'm going to die. I suppose that's good news, who cares? No one will care, no one will remember or realise I'm gone. Then again... No, No, No, No, this is a joke it's my birthday and this is a joke to get back at me for what I do to my mates. Yeah course it is..........the b.......

They had me scared for a minute. I'll just act along.
I know that I'm in the back seat and that I'm sprawled out everywhere.

Did things go according to plan:
Everything went according to plan but lack of time and insufficient hardware hampered the activity.

Future developments:
The story idea is being developed to be used in a literature context as well. Next time, though, it might be sensible to have only half the class at a time.

Aims and Objectives
Activity 2: Designing a Political Poster
To combine study of Shakespeare's *Julius Caesar* (National Curriculum Key Stage 3 English) with media awareness and the development of IT skills

Software:
WriteOn
PaintSpa
Software Production Associates

Hardware
16 RM Nimbus net
good quality printer

Project description

The class had access for two one-hour lessons to the school network of 18 Nimbus machines located in two rooms. They were given a worksheet to help with predrafting before the lesson. It explained the background to the activity: 'Brutus and his fellow conspirators had a publicity problem after they had assassinated Caesar... you have been appointed by the party to help them overcome their problem through an effective publicity campaign. It is your job to come up with an URGENTLY needed slogan and logo'.

Mostly working in pairs on the computers, each member put forward

*Brutus fREE our people.
freedom from Caesar.
Rejoice Rome is at
PEACE!*

*Be brave
Be strong
Make the right decision
Be with Brutus and co.*

" The stars in the sky
SHINE TO LIBERTY
now you have the
chance as well "

Figure 3.3 Slogans and logos

either a slogan or logo from hand-written first draft and put it on the screen. The logo was drawn first in PainSPA, saved and imported into WriteOn and combined with a slogan – making their own choice of fonts, sizes, etc. The combined work was then printed out (Figure 3.3).

Outcomes
The pupils learnt several new IT techniques (how to draw with a mouse, how to combine files) in the context of further understanding of a literature text through political slogan writing. The printouts revealed good-quality ideas.

Difficulties
Printing took a long time.

Future developments
Colour rather than monochrome printing would be beneficial. The same technique could perhaps be used for writing an advert or poem.

Case Study 2:

Activity 1: Writing Like An Estate Agent
&
Activity 2: Attempts at a Newspaper Page
Jane Carson (Headteacher),
Roselands J.M.I. School, Hoddesdon, Herts

Aims and Objectives
Activity 1: Writing Like An Estate Agent
The work was part of our topic on 'The School Environment'. Having covered quite a lot of material together, including scientific, geographical and historical aspects, the children were asked to imagine they were Estate Agents trying to 'sell' the school. What would they write ?

The Class
28 children, aged 11 years, in their final term at primary school. They were a mixed ability group of English middle-class background.

Software	Hardware
WORD for Windows	2 RM Nimbus computers
+WORDART	1 RM portable notebook
Microsoft	1 RM Multimedia computer with CD-ROM
	Deskjet b/w printer

Project Description

Organisation
This was a collaborative task with a partner to encourage a particular writing style. The idea was introduced by reading a selection of estate agents' descriptions of property. We discussed how the 'reality' may be 'exaggerated' but truth must always exist. One child brought in the estate agents' vocabulary guide as printed in a national newspaper, which some found highly amusing.

Many made use of dictionaries and the computer Thesaurus, the latter being introduced on 'Word for Windows' during this exercise.

For this particular activity the children first took notes as they walked around the building, inside and out, with their partner. These notes were re-arranged as they entered them on the computer, making full use of the re-drafting possibilities the computer facilitates. All had other tasks going on and daily basic work, so this activity mainly took place at the screen, in computer pairs.

We came together as a class to look at how to move text around in order to group similar facts. They all saved their text and then worked at WordArt for the titles. Finally printing took place whilst other work was being finished and mounted (Figure 3.4).

Two children had specific responsibility to keep a close eye on the rota and make sure all had finished one stage before anyone moved to the next. Here the laptop was very useful for those still at the drafting stage.

Note: The children usually work in twos, having a disk for each pair, so they save on 'floppy' in order to use any available machine. For ages from 5-11 years there is a clearly defined scheme of development in IT so all children can load, save and work at word processing, drawing packages, spreadsheets, data-handling packages and Logo. At any time tasks are set, a rota is kept by each machine so valuable 'hands on' time is never wasted. As each pair complete a task, or use up a time that has been specified, they save on their disk, clear the program and leave the machine, collecting the next on the list for their turn.
The laptop computer is useful for extra word processing time in class room when needed, and for me to check work at home!

Outcomes
It was evident that the children learnt a great deal from the task:

• They were able to pick up this style of writing by re-reading and adding to their work as it appeared on screen. This would have been an impossible effort on paper!

Roselands School is situated on elevated grounds on the outskirts of Hoddesdon. It is at the top of the Roselands estate. The approach is made by driving up Highwood Road. Just before you enter the school grounds you pass through a leafy drive with woods on either side. As you enter the grounds you see the infants playground which is economically sized so that it can contain a reasonable amount of children. To the left is a staff car park which holds enough cars for all the staff cars and more.

When you enter through the main entrance, on your left there is the staff relaxation room where after all the troubles of the day, the staff can unwind with a cup of Horlicks. True Relaxation!!!!

On the right come the the shouts of joy from the reception class. Further down the corridor is the kitchen which is well equipped with a freezer, oven and a sink. Next to the kitchen is the assembly hall which is painted a lovely green. The floor is not carpeted but a well kept wooden floor which is carefully looked after by the Caretaker. Further down the corridor is the library where children can choose a book to help them with their topic writing.Down the stairs and to the right is unit 2 which is reasonably sized to accommodate two classroom s which have a wet area and a craft area. Each Unit is equipped with the latest in computer technology. Moving on further down the corridor we come to Unit 3. As you walk in you immediately notice the massive display wall to your left. The unit again consists of two classrooms, a wet area, a quiet area and a craft area. Both classroom s are the proud owners of a 186 Nimbus computer, and year 6 have the latest 386 which is brilliantly up-to-date. Going outside you can see the junior play ground which is a lovely size for the children to play in. There is a white line which divides the footballers from the rest of the children. Next to the play ground is a wonderfully spacious playing field which is a lovely place for the children to play in the summer. It also makes a very good football pitch.

To the rear of the school is a swimming pool which is very well looked after and heated. It also has changing cubicles for boys and girls. A little further on we come to the exit. And that concludes our tour of Roselands School.

Figure 3.4 An example of the title work and part of the 'estate agent's' descriptive text.

- Skills in drafting and re-drafting increased as they are so much easier on a computer.
- Factual knowledge was gained in specific areas, as well as an

awareness of the importance of key-words, often coloured by the children when using the word processor.

- Children saw many of their own spelling errors when using the spell-checker, which they had to do before I came to check for other mistakes.
- Corrections in basic English – grammar, punctuation and structure – were shown individually as I corrected work on screen before it was printed.
- Awareness of the value of presentation was enhanced by the use of the computer. Choice of colours and type styles were carefully considered.
- Different papers were used to print on, e.g. marbled, sprayed.
- Much enjoyment was derived by reading each other's finished pieces.
- Parents were surprised by the range of vocabulary and persuasive voices of their offspring!
- Motivation was high. This seemed to be as a result of the task being facilitated by the use of a word processor. Also the finished product, printed with a title, looked very much like the 'real thing'!

Difficulties

We could always use more computers! Time is precious on the machines, and this is particularly true when the printing starts as well. It is vital to print through all non-teaching times, e.g. playtime, assembly, E.P., class tests, etc.

We did not have a colour printer to hand and made use of our black and white. Results would have been further enhanced with diagrams and drawings by combining packages but we ran out of time!

Future developments

This approach could be used in other topic areas or to encourage other specific 'types' of writing. It could be further developed with pictures, maps, plans and measuring, thus incorporating areas of maths.

Aims and Objectives

Activity 2: Attempts at a Newspaper Page

The work was part of our topic on 'Rivers'. Having covered quite a lot of material together, including scientific, geographical and historical aspects, the children were asked to present their findings on 'Pollution'. We aimed to make them more aware of their surroundings and man's abuse of the natural world.

Software:
NewSPA
Software Production Associates

Hardware
1 RM Nimbus computers
1Integrex 132 colour printer –
series 1

Project description

Organisation
This was a collaborative task with a partner to expand the use of programs already well known to the children: WriteOn and PaintSPA. NewSPA combines the two.
The idea of creating a newspaper page was introduced by reading a

Green...

22,May 1995   25p

GREEN ALGAE STRIKES THE THAMES

The banks of the River Thames in London gave way yesterday,due to the huge amount of monsterous green algae.This caused distress among the nearby residents.So far only three minor injuries have been reported,but many homes have been ruined.

Major Oil Spillage In North Sea!

Last night a major oil spillage occured when one of the worlds largest tankers collided in dense fog with an American Tug-boat.No injuries have been reported yet,although many are feared missing.
No oil has reached land,but it is a race against time to break it up so it pollutes no more sea and doesn't reach land.

The crude oil is highly dangerous to all wildlife so it is important that it is removed.The removal of this oil is an expensive and slow process,but it has to be done.
C.C Tankers (The makers of the tanker involved) have said that they are willing to pay for all of the costs,but this money will not help the wildlife already in danger.

Figure 3.5 The Pollution Report

GREEN

Insects that love pollution:

THE MAGAZINE THAT CARES

The Pollution Scheme..

Margaret Thatcher said yesterday in the House of Lords that she was going to sp--end £8 million on cleaning up British rivers.The scheme will be debated in the House of Lords on Monday.We asked Neil Kinnock what he thought about the so ca--lled 'Pollution Scheme'.He hastily rep--lied,"I personally think that the sche--me will make no difference to the poll--ution in today's rivers".The leader of the 'Green' party said"If the scheme go--es ahead I will rejoice,but there is a 60 percent chance it won't."

POLLUTION DAMAGE

Different types of pollution damage different thin--gs.C.F.C's (clorafloracarbons) are harmful towards our ozone layer,these are found in many aerosoles. Rubbish pollution is harmful to different types of wildlife,it is caused by man and could be stopped. Fertilizers used on crops often pollute our rivers and get into animals foods.Our rivers get polluted by sewage from sewage farms and the beaches get polluted from rubbish.Oil slicks can create great pr--oblems for our wildlife,and can be hard to remove.

selection of newspaper and magazine pages. Having looked at their layouts I introduced the software and the concept of editor, reporter, and illustrator, relating these to the programs already known. The children planned their separate items and how they would present them.

All had other tasks going on and daily basic work, so this activity mainly took place at the screen, in computer pairs.

Note: See Activity 1 for the way the class was organised.

Outcomes

It was evident that the children learnt a great deal from the task. Some completed a 'whole' page. The example shows the degree of achievement (Figure 3.5). A great variety of experimentation took place.

Many separate items had to be combined so the task demanded competent use of disk handling and constant reviewing of size and layout of the page.

Those who didn't achieve the whole page had pieces on WriteOn or PaintSPA they could still print out, so everyone had something to show!

Difficulties

There was limited overall success as the task demanded so much time – we could always use more computers !

Time is precious on the machines, and this is particularly true when the printing starts as well. It is vital to print during all non-teaching times, e.g. playtime, assembly, PE, class tests.

A few were rather daunted by the size of the task and chose to limit themselves to one article, rather than a page.

Future Developments

This approach has been used in other topic areas and was successful. It could be more successful if the children were in bigger groups and had defined tasks to produce one piece for the total page. The editor would need to be highly organised and review the page layout regularly.

Chapter 4

Electronic communication

Niki Davis
with Colin Kirkman, Hugh McShane, Mike Ounsworth and David
Vipond

Description of a key application

In this chapter we take electronic communication to be the use of computers to communicate outside the classroom, either to work with others or to obtain information. Although this excludes a range of services based on normal telephones or satellites there has been little use of such services in compulsory education so little current practice is excluded. Electronic communication can best be described as a range of services available to individuals and institutions. They fall into two groups: networked services and point-to-point services.

Networked services
The fundamental service used in electronic communication is electronic mail. This service transmits word-processed messages to an electronic address anywhere in the world. Multiple recipients are as easy as one and the mail can get there almost immediately, if the recipient is connected on-line to receive it. If not the message waits until the recipient connects to their host computer.

Computer Conferencing is slightly different in that the messages on a topic are arranged into a conference and any participant can read and add messages. It isn't necessary to have the address for others, instead all choose to look at all the messages and join in. For example, one international conference, called 'comp.edu', is about computers in education for teachers or school students around the world and has many participants in many countries, especially USA and Australia.

Electronic communication can also be used to access information. Campus 2000 has several databases and notice-boards provided by participants which can be searched and that information may be down-loaded to disk. Services which provide extensive gateways, such as JANET and BITNET, may be viewed as one vast interconnected network. The term 'the Internet' is often used to refer to these interconnected services available around the world. Databases are available on many host computers and because of their interconnection vast quantities of information (uncensored) are available. However, care should be exercised in the use of information obtained in this way. It is uncensored, depending only on the skill and moral values of the individual who provided it.

Point-to-point services

Bulletin boards provide services similar to those above for networked services, especially notice-boards and databases. Users connect directly to a computer to view the information, instead of using an intermediate host computer.

Desk Top Conferencing (DTC) is completely different. It is more like communication over the phone than electronic mail. It uses a pair of ISDN (Integrated Services Digital Network) telephone lines to link participants at either end (point to point), sharing both voice and computer systems. Teacher and student can run the same software together, see the same screen, discuss it and even key in changes. In addition a 'flipchart' facility is available and file transfer is extremely quick. To establish a link one participant simply dials up the computer system and phone at the other end using the ISDN lines, which are part of the ordinary UK phone network. They then have a dedicated line for the duration of the call over which they can talk to each other and a second line which displays the graphics and text of one of the computer systems on the screens at both ends. The call charge is the same as that incurred for the telephone in the UK for each phone line in use. The audio and data phone lines may be used separately or together.

Electronic communication available in the UK

The services available to education in the UK have varied since their inception in the early 1980s. They are either networked services with one or more host computers or services used between two points. We will consider networked systems first.

For compulsory education there is the Campus 2000 system available anywhere in the UK for the cost of a local phone call and paid for by monthly (previously annual) subscription by institutions. The institution is now allocated two identities for all users in the institution (previously one). Campus 2000 provides central Telecom Gold electronic mail, some databases created and updated by volunteers or sponsors and computer conferencing. Additional services may also be purchased. For example, the remains of the viewdata system, Prestel Education, and gateways to services such as ECCTIS, which provides information on courses in UK further and higher education. There are also a few local systems available within a region, frequently run in association with the local education authority.

Services outside the UK such as Bitnet are now available through gateway services, but do not have local call access nationally. These are predominantly American and can appear culturally biased to UK users.

For higher education and research the Joint Academic Network (JANET), funded by the Department for Education, provides national electronic links between universities plus gateways to other services including networks in other countries. This service is free to universities, but they must manage the mail distribution and user support themselves. A wider band network, SuperJANET, is now also being installed.

Point-to-point electronic communication is also available. Any individual or institution could make their computer available to outside users by attaching a modem. A few do so to provide information on bulletin boards. A new form of digital telephone line called ISDN (Integrated Services Digital Network) is coming into service for point-to-point communication. These lines have at least twice the band width of ordinary phone lines and, as they are digital, the signal has no errors. They can carry both voice and computer information, including video, relatively easily for any sector of education. In future, these lines may also permit up to ten points to be connected together at one time.

The potential of electronic communication

The potential of electronic communication is related to its potential audience: it is world wide. Where students are given access, they can ignore the walls of the classroom and make direct contact with others across the world for collaborative work and in so doing appreciate the differences in culture and yet the similarity of people. Communication is a central activity within education and thus electronic communication can be applied to almost any area. Fundamental aspects are: written communication, presentation of information for different audiences and/or research. The activity is essentially pupil-centred and mixed ability. Group work is hard to avoid, unless bibliographic research is the only activity. Communication with those outside the classroom is tremendously motivating for both pupils and teacher and this to a large extent justifies the extra time and effort spent on the process (Coyle and

44

Harrison, 1993).

Electronic communication also has an important benefit for those with communication difficulties. While such people have many reasons for their difficulty electronic communication can provide them with an important channel. Their context is often so different from that of a normal pupil that people with whom they communicate will have made many assumptions before the first message is received. Prejudice arises between cultures. Electronic communication removes this bias while being particularly suited to their strengths. For example, one of the first electronic mail projects in Northern Ireland had the important side-effect of increasing the integration of the pupils from a special school with their local schools.

Students can also become apprentices in a number of fields: collecting data and interpreting it with other pupils and scientists; working with an author to write novels; collecting articles and producing a newspaper (see later case study); in humanities using real information sources provided by pupils in another location and returning the favour for those pupils (see later case study). The inter-connection of learners provides them with an audience for whom they will write, possibly in a target language which is that of their audience, but not their own. While these activities are also possible using tradi-tional post or visits, the timeliness of the communication permits learning to take place within the attention span of the pupils and the school timetable. Information provided by pupils in another location is not mediated by the publishing process and such 'raw' data is frequently more relevant to the pupils than that in a textbook. Where time permits additional questions can be posed to explore the data and correct misunderstandings.

The style of communicating through electronic mail or computer conferencing where messages are read, an answer composed and returned without the recipient waiting around permits the process to become more reflective. The students can review their next communica-tion for half an hour if they wish, and yet the communication remains timely in a way that is rare with letters. Similarly shy participants may be facilitated because they do not have to confront their audience in person. For point-to-point communication such as DeskTop Conferencing the last point does not apply. Instead the communication process becomes intense with participants focusing on both the imme-diate changes visible on the computer screen and the personal contact of the voice (Davis, 1994).

Electronic communication has potential benefits for teachers and teacher education (Meadows, 1992). It permits collaboration across distant schools and with those in higher education. Discussion groups on the Internet hold a large volume of discussion about curriculum, educational practice and theories. Such discussion can provide a wider range of viewpoints and suggestions for developments or solutions to common problems. However as they are not edited they require sifting.

It is also important for the reader to note that electronic communication does not easily fit in with traditional classroom practice:

○ 'By its very nature classroom use of communication technology is contrary to the notion that learning occurs in isolation and is teacher-centred. For effective employment of this technology, teachers must be comfortable with the technology itself, value its potential, be process oriented, work co-operatively, and allow students to do the same.'

(Szymanski *et al.,* 1993)

Like most applications used within computer-based learning, electronic communications will support the teachers who wish to move into a support role and permit their pupils to develop autonomy and information skills rather than absorb knowledge under the teachers' direct mediation. Unlike other applications it is almost impossible to use it without such an approach.

Research on the effectiveness of electronic communication

There has been relatively little hard research into the benefits of electronic communication. Collis (1992) reviewed the evaluation strategies described in more than 120 projects involving telecommunications for distributed learning at the secondary level and concluded that 'evaluation is apparently difficult to do'. Of those projects which did attempt evaluation most was impressionistic or attitudinal. Collis (1993) discusses these difficulties and suggests a strategy related to success indicators (long and short term; planned and unplanned) and the relation between these and the assumptions and observed characteristics of the context. It is recognised that multi-site implementations make evaluation exceedingly complex especially as it must be related to the needs at each site and these inevitably over time . Having acknowledged these difficulties the following case studies will attempt to both evaluate and describe the use of electronic communication in education.

The case studies

Three case studies have been chosen to illustrate the potential of electronic communications in education. The first highlights both multicultural education and the sharing of resources across countries developed through Roger Austin's (1990) project: Education for Mutual Understanding. The second highlights bringing primary children in small schools together. Finally we review a modern languages Newspaper Day in which electronic communications provides important sources and context material in modern foreign languages. Many other projects could have been chosen. Those which involve initial teacher education provide particularly strong cases for the apprenticeship model for both student teacher, collaborating staff, and students in school; see, for example, Meadows (1992).

The European Studies Project is a strong example of international collaboration which serves educational purposes. Its originator, Dr Roger Austin of the University of Ulster's European Telecommunications Centre, continues to spread the work across and within countries and to develop associated media with support from national PTT companies, including British Telecom. The project started within the theme of 'education for mutual understanding' and took the conflicts in Ireland and Belgium as a focus within history and geography. Eighteen schools (6 Northern Ireland, 6 English and 6 in the Republic of Ireland) took part in the 11–16 programme. All schools had access to a Campus 2000 subscription as well as software for word processing, database work and newspaper generators. E–mail was the main medium for communication alongside an exchange of audio and videotapes and written material. All schools received considerable in-service and planning support from Dr Austin and the 11–16 group met annually at an Irish centre in Belgium. Seven modules of work have been developed across 3 years. They start with a local focus in the first year, for example:

'My Community'

moving to wider issues in year two,

'Our shared environment'

and into more sensitive questions in year three,

'Attitudes to conflict – a case study of Ireland, Britain and Europe 1914–1916'.

With considerable effort this was carefully integrated into examination courses in all three countries. Pupils working in local groups shared their reports and chat sessions across all schools by e-mail and supplemented them with other material by post, for example a video 'Belfast for Beginners.'

A similar programme has taken place for 16–18-year-old pupils across schools in France and Germany in addition to the original three countries and here the pupils have expressed their appreciation for the medium.

The speed and potential immediacy of information regardless of distance are an important motivator and provide participants with an audience which improves relevance of the work, access to resources and self-esteem. Issues relating to equal opportunities in a multi-cultural context can be addressed through sharing work outside the institution, especially across borders. Time differences can be overcome due to the way in which messages can be stored until 'called' for and still electronic communication are fast enough to support group discussions. This is important across both time zones and timetables. The ease and availability of information for redistribution and re-working is clearly important to some projects too. Probably the most important aim shared by teachers who use electronic communication is education for mutual understanding in a world torn by conflict. While such a right is not as important as that of health care, it could be an important infrastructure to assist new generations to overcome prejudice.

Summary

Those who benefit from electronic communication appear to be:

- distributed people or organisations;
- those keen to gain experience outside their location and who are prepared to use a flexible learning strategy;
- distance learners who want to communicate;
- people with a communications disadvantage;
- centres keen to disseminate work;
- people willing to provide mutual self help and facilitate social change.

The points learned so far relate to the need to communicate:

- the ease of access;
- the development of group work;
- use of an impoverished medium of communication.

These factors make electronic communication difficult for the ordinary use in education and mean that most successful projects are very closely related to the need for electronic communication to overcome other problems. In future a variety of multi-media telecommunications applications will probably develop, related to the leisure industry. The factors relating to today's simple systems will remain important if valuable educational applications are to become embedded in the curriculum, especially equality of access, standardisation of protocols and staff

development. One step might be to address the need to support student teachers in school based training by using electronic communication, thus raising awareness of its value within the teaching force.

The benefits from telematics·were learned before the start of the projects described here, but they continue to be true. The speed and potential immediacy of information regardless of distance are an important motivator and provide participants with an audience which improves relevance of the work, access to resources and self-esteem. Equal opportunities, culture and global issues can be addressed through sharing work outside the institution, especially when it is across borders (Davis, 1988, 1993). Time differences can be overcome due to the way in which messages can be stored until 'called' for and yet remains fast enough to support group discussions. This is important across both time zones and timetables. The ease and availability of information for redistribution and re-working is clearly important to some projects too. For example, the Newspaper days remain popular since their inception many years ago with support from the Times Newspaper and access to professional sources of up-to-the-minute 'raw news'.

Probably the most important aim shared by teachers who use telematics is education for mutual understanding in a world torn by conflict. The World Conference on Children's Rights held in Exeter in 1992 debated a proposition that children should have a right to computer-mediated communications, rather than pay the commercial rates. The electronic and face-to-face debate conceded that such a right was not as important as for health but that it could be an important infrastructure to assist new generations to overcome prejudice.

Electronic communications must have the greatest potential of all computer-based learning. After all these communication channels can carry almost any other form of communication including computer-based learning anywhere in the world, used either instantly or at a time and place to suit the learner. However, such potential is accompanied by increased practical difficulties. The information communicated should be both timely and relevant to be of value and there are issues relating to access and collaboration across timetables and cultures. As this chapter has illustrated (see Case Studies 1 to 3) teachers and learners have enthusiastically participated in computer-based learning though electronic communication. Team spirit within schools and across countries has led to the development of knowledge and skills which are greatly valued within education. However, long-term use of electronic communications is a more difficult development of awareness among student teachers.

Case Study 1:

European Studies (16–18) Project 1987–93
Hugh McShane
Sacred Heart Grammar School, Newry.

Project Aims and Objectives
As part of its commitment to helping young people in Northern
Ireland to broaden their educational experience as European citi-
zens, the Department of Education ran a pilot project in 1987 to link
students from Northern Ireland with those in Belgium. The project
schools invited to participate, Banbridge Academy and Sacred
Heart Grammar School, Newry, received full financial support from
both the Central Bureau for Educational Exchanges and Visits and
from the Commission for the European Communities.
The purpose of the pilot project was to provide regular opportunities for young people:

• To explore, through curriculum contact, the shared experience
  and rich diversity of their heritage in the context of Europe.
• To become acquainted with the work of political and economic
  institutions, especially those of the European Community.
• To acquire a better understanding of their own society through a
  comparative study of situations elsewhere in Europe.
• To use IT across European frontiers as an aid to investigation
  and communication, alongside more traditional methods such
  as telephone, audio cassette, letter post and personal contact.

The Class/Students
Lower sixth-form (aged 17) , most had basic IT skills.

Software	Hardware
Campus 2000; terminal software;	a standard educational computer networked electronic communications with central computer in London
Campus 2000 in association with BT	*Minimum:* one mail box per school and a phone line accessible by the teacher only
annual subscription of £300 plus local phone charges	*Ideally:* access in area used by pupils in normal and study time. Also access from home with fast error checking modems and easy to use software for word processing and terminal emulation Both teacher and pupils to have individual mail boxes.

a word-processing package   modem, printer, phone line

Project Description:

Development
In the developmental phase of the project, schools were linked together for joint work. Wherever possible, schools were asked to try to ensure that the following conditions were met, to increase the chances of successful inter-school contact:

- Contact should be long term rather than short term.
- Contact should be co-operative rather than competitive and between participants of equal status. In the case of the two Northern Ireland schools, pupils were studying A Level, were Lower sixth-form (aged 17) and most had basic IT skills.
- Contact should be purposeful and lead to a sense of shared experience, between groups rather than individuals.

Since 1987 the link between the two schools in Northern Ireland and other countries has been extended to include the Republic of Ireland, England, France and Germany, as well as Belgium. The present grouping of 10 schools allows for a wide national and cultural range of partners without overwhelming students with too many contacts.

The Place of Information Technology in the 16–18 Project.
In 1987 the focus was very strongly on Electronic Mail, using Campus 2000 as the channel by which participating schools exchanged reports on the topics they had researched. Since 1987 computer conferencing has proved to be a valuable addition to the channel of communication, allowing students to come together at an agreed time to discuss their research findings. Schools have also made use of video material filmed by students. These have either been sent as complete programmes to linked schools or as contributions to satellite broadcasts which the Project has co-ordinated. In 1990 two programmes based entirely on video reports sent in by the project schools were produced for the Olympus Satellite. By 1991 we were able to receive the Astra Satellite and three programmes were produced for Channel E. The combination of research presented via electronic mail with the colour and texture of video reports has proven to be very motivational for students.

Organisation
In the first year of the project, European Studies was not timetabled. We selected a group of 12 students from the lower sixth-form, all of whom were voluntary participants, committed, motivated and enthusiastic.

Most had only basic IT skills and, in fact, this was not one of the criteria for selection. The group worked during free periods, lunch time and after school. We were able to locate the computer and telephone line in a room where students could have regular access, allowing them to decide when they would engage in the IT aspect of the project.

Exchanges through the medium of electronic mail constituted a swift and effective means of communication. Messages could be sent instantaneously to one or more recipients and the system allowed for information to be stored in a filing area allocated to each mailbox. Communications could be sent on-line by typing in text after the log-on sequence was completed. Typing on-line was adequate for short messages but it must be remembered that telephone charges are incurred while subscribers are on-line and a much more cost-effective method was to prepare reports on disk and upload them into the system. Similarly, it is much cheaper to download incoming messages onto disk and print them out subsequently, rather than printing while on-line. This was the usual method but we did occasionally use the on-line method as a means of bringing students together so that they had that important experience of live, personal contact with their counterparts in Banbridge and in Leuven. I feel that this was useful as it brought an exciting, novel experience to the students at a time when e-mail was relatively new and gave the students a feeling that they were part of the frontier in IT. With the active support of our IT Department, students were able to master more sophisticated techniques of uploading, downloading and spooling of text as the year progressed.

In later years students used Caucus conferencing, which allows groups of students to work together on a common theme and respond to each other's thoughts and ideas. Participants do not need to be involved, or on-line at the same time. They can review the progress of the discussion and make a contribution any time of the day.

Once students became familiar with the basic procedures associated with E-mail we devised a strategy by which students took turns logging on at a regular time each day, downloading material, making any immediate responses necessary and printing out messages for distribution to students within the group. At the same time material prepared on disk could be uploaded and transmitted. When the group met as a whole, students working on specific topics could update others of the group on materials sent or received during the previous week.

Difficulties
One of the principal causes of disappointment and loss of motivation in the use of E-mail is the failure of schools to deliver messages and

reports on time or to participate actively and regularly in the process. In 1987 the schools involved were highly motivated, responsive and committed to regular communication. This was vital. I feel that this helped maintain the momentum necessary for success. There were occasional technical hitches but the support from the project office was such that continuity and regularity of contact was quickly restored.

Outcomes
Pupils who previously were uncomfortable and fearful when confronted by the prospect of IT activity gained in confidence from their success in E-mail and their involvement helped break down the psychological barriers sometimes associated with IT. Those students who already had IT skills gained from the experience of helping their classmates come to terms with the skills and this had the effect of bonding the group closer together.

In the years since 1987 the use of video communication and fax machines has to some extent reduced the impact of E-mail but it remains a central feature of the communication process within the European Studies Project. The need for deadlines to be met and for students to master fairly quickly the E-mail procedure enhanced the learning experience for the pupils, particularly as they were excited by the technology which could on the one hand bring them into direct contact through the on-line method and also allow them to send and receive detailed and meaningful information at a more leisurely pace through the mailbox system.

Pupils who put themselves forward for participation in the project were initially motivated by the issues, by the interest in the concept of Europe and by the prospect of meeting other young Europeans personally at the residential conference but I believe that E-mail has played an important role in helping students develop a positive and informed pre-residential relationship with their counterparts in other parts of Europe.

Future Development
We would hope to extend involvement in the project to a larger number of sixth-form students and to involve pupils in the Junior School. At the moment the group consists of a small number of pupils in the Senior School.

Case Study 2:

E-mail days for small schools
David Vipond
Lerryn Church of England Junior and Infants School, Cornwall

Project Aims And Objectives
The aim of the project was to permit small numbers of pupils scattered across the UK in small schools to share their work and so gain not only a large number of co-pupils but also to increase their understanding of geography and different cultures of the UK.
The objective was to research the playground games played on the 1st May and to share this data and work on it across the schools with other pupils.

The Class/Students
15 junior school pupils from 9 to 12 years old, mixed ability and gender, in a small rural school.
Most of the 15 primary schools participating were rural but a few were inner city schools, all with less than 5 teachers. This report focuses on one of the 15.

Software:
Campus 2000;
terminal software;

Campus 2000 in association with BT

annual subscription of £100 plus local phone charges

Word Wise word processor

Computer Concepts

Hardware
BBC Master + networked electronic communications with central computer in London
Minimum: one mail box per school and a phone line accessible by the teacher only
Ideally: access in area used by pupils in normal and study time. Also access from home with fast error checking modems and easy-to-use software for word processing and terminal emulation
Both teacher and pupils to have individual mail boxes.
modem, printer, phone line

Project Description

Organisation
The project was co-ordinated centrally by Exeter University. Teachers had received two day's in-service training using Campus 2000 at BT's Goonhilly Earth Station in Cornwall.

54

Most of our work is topic based, so a topic was designed around the theme of children's games. Discussion took place in our classroom about the games that were played during playtimes. From the children came the idea to do an in-school survey of the games played. This information was turned into graph work showing the popularity of games. Many of the games played by the children were new to me, so the children undertook the task of making illustrated rule books to show how the games were played. The children read one another's rule books and they were asked to look for common features in the games. Working in groups the children then sorted the games into categories by themselves. Class discussion took place about the various categories. Some category headings were common but others, although containing the same kind of game, were different. These headings were: pretending, tig, football, rounders, ball games, skipping, jumping, hiding and (for games that fitted none of those categories) other.

On the day of the survey, two children made a record of all the games that were played. This information was typed into a file and sent to Exeter using E-mail. The information sent to our mail box that had come from other schools via Exeter was down-loaded onto disk. The children printed out the information received and cut out the information provided by individual schools. Much interest was shown in the names of these schools, and the children spent a lot of time finding them on road atlases. A large map of Great Britain was drawn and displayed on the wall. Using mapping pins the children pinpointed the position of the schools. From the pins showing the places pieces of cotton were led to the section on the display boards and there the children pinned up the games that had been played in those schools.

Further work followed using the computer data handling package Key. The results from the survey were entered into the computer which allowed the children to interrogate the data further and allowed them to use the computer to create bar-charts and pie-charts to display the data.

Lerryn received this message from Stokeinteignhead in Devon:

'we have played games (see below, more info tomorrow)
Spot – a football game
Ghost busters – pretend game
Handstands
Rainbow Towers
Count Duckula
Non-stop rounders.'

(first published in *Microscope*, **32**, p.29)

Outcomes
The children found the project very simulating and were keen to communicate with their fellow researchers. The teacher continued the research and found the data provided a remarkable contrast with that gathered 20 years before by Clive Opie (Opie and Opie, 1969). Playground games were not nearly so regional and the influence of TV was obvious.

The children's remarks also clearly showed that their concept of the UK had grown. The map had real meaning for them despite the fact that several had never left Cornwall. They found this apprenticeship model of research easy and with assistance from the teacher were able to find sensible answers to questions asked of the database.

The immediacy of the events provide both important stimulation for the pupils and control for the teacher. The relevance and timeliness of information from other children was absorbing. The map put their collaborators in context and added a geographic aspect.

Difficulties

Conceptual
Teachers found the concepts behind electronic communication difficult. The passage of messages to and from a central computer via a local phone number was difficult to understand and the need for clean files rather than apparently similar word-processed documents poorly understood. Such technical concepts should not be important but were in this context.

Organisational
The plan went well on the day. The continuation of electronic communications was disappointingly rare.

Technical
Lines were noisy at times leading to corrupted messages. These were re-transmitted, but such work was tedious rather than exciting.

Future Developments

• This school wanted to repeat the activity with a difference focus each term, but there was no consensus among the group. Similarly no one wanted to take over the co-ordinating role played by the university.
• The event could be run in a similar way each year with a different group of students.
• The database aspect had not been designed in and was an optional extension.

Case Study 3:

Modern Foreign Languages Newspaper Day
Colin Kirkman (IT), Mike Ounsworth (MFL)
St Peter's High School, Exeter

Project Aims And Objectives
The object was to produce a newspaper in a range of modern foreign languages. Some source material provide by E-mail on the day by a group of A-level students who formed the national Newsday Newsdesk in Cleveland.

This activity aimed to use languages for real purposes, working from authentic materials, and also to stretch the students' IT skills and organisational ability.

The Class/Students
22 students chosen for language ability from three Y10 classes. Mixed gender and social background from a small city's comprehensive school.

Software

Campus 2000;
terminal software;

Campus 2000 in association with BT

annual subscription of £365 plus local phone charges

DTP software.
word processing software
clip art and images

Hardware

Archimedes network + networked electronic communications with central computer in London
Minimum: one mail box per school and a phone line accessible by the teacher only
Ideally: access in area used by pupils in normal and study time. Also access from home with fast error checking modems and easy to use software for word processing and terminal emulation
Both teacher and pupils to have individual mail boxes.

modem, printer, phone line
Teletel, the national German electronic network, and Italian TV
Scanner, Ion camera, clip art and images

Project Description

Organisation

The induction day included a talk by a representative of a local newspaper. This awareness of style, layout and organisation was important. A student editor and two subeditors were appointed to oversee and run the project. Much of the afternoon of the induction day was spent working out systems and lines of communication to enable effective control of newspaper production. The university link person provided useful support leading up to the event and kept busy teachers' minds focused on the forthcoming event.

The computer room was taken over for the day by this project. Students who participated started with a low level of IT skill. The initial approach was sufficient for all pupils to gain proficiency in text and filing operations. Students has already prepared some written materials as part of their language preparation, so this was used as a basis for Desk Top Publishing. Students off site conducted interviews with native speakers and E-mailed their reports to the school. We also looked at controlling the style and layout of pages, and the capture and incorporation of graphics. Further acquisition of IT skills was on a need to know basis and so was relevant to each pupil's situation.

The first challenge of the day itself was to handle the large quantity of electronic mail fed to us. This involved a high level of technical and linguistic skill. The student teachers acted as assistants advising on composition and helping with proof reading.

Outcomes

A steady stream of visitors and helpers visited throughout the day to observe the development of the newspaper. Several commented on the calm, organised and hard-working environment. The pupils concerned demonstrated a high (and surprising) degree of sophistication and competence in such areas as scanning screens for newsworthy items, choosing items to work on directly in the foreign language and editing them down without passing through the medium of English. The team spirit and achievement of the goal to publish a newspaper entirely in modern foreign languages was very motivating. Pupils begin to see that they can have access to the real world of languages used for real purposes, not merely chunks of discourse taken from a textbook.

Evaluation was carried out by a student teacher's questionnaire and by the MFL teacher's observation of work in progress and conversation afterwards. 'When can we do it again?' was a constant question.

Motivating factors
Communication technology is one of the few ways to make external sources of input really meaningful in the confines of a Languages classroom. Pupils begin to see that they can have access to the real world of languages used for real purposes. One student teacher reported:

> 'I personally think that a Newspaper Day is a super idea, and I can say with absolute certainty that the pupils really enjoyed it. The questionnaires I gave out reflected this. We student teachers needed more guidance on how much we were allowed to help, especially given the time pressures and motivation of the pupils.'

Difficulties

Conceptual
The level of MFL language expected by A-level students in Cleveland of their younger Y10 students was rather high.

Organisational
The main problems were non-receipt of specimen materials until a very late stage and these were mainly for an English newspaper day.

Technical
Duplicate files received caused some confusion but the filtering and computer network directories set up for incoming, draft and final materials solved many of the potential problems.

The disruption caused by taking a whole day off timetable was unfortunate, but was clearly outweighed by the gains.

Future Developments

- Teachers' levels of awareness of the possibilities offered by IT have been raised and it is hoped that we will be able to incorporate more IT into MFL.
- We will operate at a lower language level and have more advance preparation including a visit to a newspaper.
- We would want the same and other pupils doing more of this activity within class and at lunch times on an *ad hoc* basis.
- There needs to be more cross-curriculum integration. The fact Y10 were already involved in newspaper production for English was valuable.

Chapter 5
Using graphics packages

Simon FitzPatrick
with Keith Clark, Lesley O' Callaghan and Mark Rogers

This chapter looks at the relevance and place of computer graphics within the curriculum, and includes three examples of computer-based graphics activities. The case studies do not cover the full spectrum of use, rather they represent a 'snapshot' of current developments. What they do show is the breadth and scope of a tool that is used in a huge variety of situations. The key factor is the amount of imagination and creative thinking that has gone into the construction of a positive learning experience. These examples are taken from a North-amptonshire secondary school, well endowed with 'technology'; and a Northamptonshire Further Education college, using older resources. In all three cases we are dealing with the learning process, rather than the product. The means by which the objective is achieved, becomes some-what secondary.

Developments in technology continue at a pace which astounds close followers of the industry, yet it is fair to say that education remains a rather quiet backwater. There are many reasons for this, including the continuing resistance of teachers to adapt to the new technologies, but perhaps the main reasons are cost and time: there are few schools in a position to replace their hard-won desktop computers with the latest multimedia workstations. Despite huge advances in software design and performance, many teachers have bemoaned the lack of time they have to study and explore a package in detail. Often, a change in hardware or software is going to have considerable repercussions on teaching and learning strategies. The case study material will reflect both sides of the technological divide, but at this stage it may be worth taking a brief look at the current state of play, and to reflect on the implications for educationalists.

Computer graphics – A good thing?

It is generally accepted that computer graphics are 'a good thing' – yet, arguments still rage over whether students using computers can produce 'art', and some observers suggest that the technology 'produces' the image. Indeed computer graphics can be seen as a threat to the use of traditional techniques. Occasionally, computer graphics is used as an ideal method for keeping students quiet, others see it as an ideal 'carrot': 'finish your work, and you can draw on the computer'. We must be careful to ensure that technology is placed within its correct context – it must act as a complementary aid to the tools that the tutor has at his or her disposal.

Graphics packages may be seen as just one more medium for student use although Tony Hodgson would argue that these new tools may suggest and lead to new methods of working (Hodgson *et al.*, 1993). One of the positive characteristics of graphics packages is that it does not require a high IT entry skill level. Outcomes from initial experimenting and the 'play' aspect will assist the future growth of IT skills and competencies, as well as developing the user's confidence in operating the system. Experimentation is perhaps a key word here, as the nature of the computer, with its storage retrieval facility, ensures that the user is encouraged to develop an idea, secure in the knowledge that the original may be kept safe, and copies can be distorted beyond all recognition. Case Study 3 shows clearly the advantages of having a 'master copy', which is then manipulated by students, who are happy to return to the tutor to collect a fresh 'master' when an experiment goes awry. Another popular example is the 'altering' of replica pictures: the computer allows the easy substitution of alternative colours and textures, giving the user a greater degree of insight into the composition of the original.

High levels of presentation and output are strong motivators for all age groups. In certain situations, the use of a computer can actually make a task easier, and the user may be able to achieve more acceptable results than with a more traditional medium, thus enhancing motivation. This is particularly true in the case of tasks with a high degree of co-ordination skills – the precision and accuracy of a graphics package can produce real advantages. A simple example would be a room-planning exercise, where the user may find that copying, pasting, moving and re-sizing parts of the image are vital, as there is no pressure to ensure that the plan is completed at the first attempt. I have used the example of kitchen design services, where the 'virtual' kitchen can be created on-screen, and then manipulated.

The development of peripheral equipment – including digitisers, screen grabbers and scanning equipment – has also affected perceptions of 'art educators'. It is now possible to take an image from one medium and manipulate it beyond all recognition. Or, by using packages which mimic traditional techniques the student can 'paint' in the style of the Impressionist, for example. Cooper(1990) suggests that such processes give the art teacher the ability to extend the historical and cultural awareness of pupils by engaging them in a parallel exercise, providing a means whereby image construction and composition can be examined and re-examined in the light of this 'parallel' experience.

The truly flexible nature of the computer graphics application has far-reaching implications beyond art and into the entire curriculum – there are few instances where creative use of a package fails to enhance the student's or pupil's work. Projects and assignments can be enhanced by colourful, visual additions, from simple front-sheets, to complex decoration of charts. This flexibility allows the teacher many opportunities for developing a whole range of learning situations across the curriculum.

Software developments

A major development in computer graphics has been the introduction of drawing packages as alternatives to painting packages. This shift from the pixel-based image to the object-oriented illustration is significant. The change has affected the skills required of a user: the traditional paint program bore a direct resemblance to using the paintbrush or pencil, and the toolboxes reflected these traditional tools. This is not so in draw packages; here the user arranges objects. In practical terms, this has enhanced the division between the 'artist' and the 'designer'.

Applications such as Paintspa and MacPaint have an immediacy lacking in the new draw packages such as Coreldraw, Freehand, or Illustrator and these latter packages place heavy demands on hardware, memory and processor performance in particular. Paintspa has proved itself an ideal tool right across the curriculum and the age range, particularly as it has now become part of a suite of inter-linked applications, including 'slideshow' facilities. These include 'Pagelink', a hypertext-type extension that allows users to navigate through a number of images, via a series of decision-making screens; and 'Newspa', a simple DTP system.

More recent developments of the painting package have tended to be directed at younger age groups, where the user is more interested in the direct correlation between using an input device such as a mouse, and the effect on-screen. An interesting recent package is 'KidPix', a simple enough painting package, aimed at younger age groups, and beginning to attract support in schools. It attaches a sound to each particular tool and effect, and the user can also record and save a sound to a picture. The package has a variety of special effects, for example the 'dynamite' effect, which 'blows up' the picture as a means of erasing it. It too has a 'slideshow' facility(see also Powerpoint and Persuasion) and the facility to show 'Quicktime' video clips in the picture.

The package features an extensive array of clip-art pictures and symbols. Clip-art is seen by many as a non-attributable accessory, which devalues the design and manipulation process. This argument is perhaps best seen in the context of the 'art' student, where evidence of originality and creativity is paramount. For the graphic designer, CAD user or technical designers a clip-art library is a legitimate tool. In this setting, the boundaries are clear: for 'KidPix' the inclusion of ready-made pictures enhances the program – children in the target age range enjoy the chance to build and embellish their stories without struggling to comprehend all functions of the toolbox. Paint packages are examples of applications which are easy to use 'out of the box', yet can develop along with the user; a novice can achieve a result very quickly. Another paint package of interest is Painter, from Fractal Design. In this package the paint analogy is taken to its logical conclusion, and the user is provided with a comprehensive set of chalks, crayons, felt pens, etc. with 'smudge' and 'water' effects. When combined with textured 'surfaces', the product is strikingly similar to the real thing! This effect is further enhanced through the use of alternative input devices, especially graphics tablets.

Painter costs around £200.00 for a single user copy and has high hardware demands and for these reasons will find limited educational use, unlike Claris Works (see Case Studies 2 and 3). Strictly speaking this is an integrated package, but the graphics facilities are interesting. There are a number of packages of this type currently on the market – in the past they were seen very much as poor relations of the mainstream software market, but they have become an important part of the home computer market. In addition Computer Aided Design (CAD) packages, modelling and simulation packages, although still expensive and hardware-hungry, are now within the reach of education users. One cannot do full justice to the entire field which is designing, drawing and painting with computers within an article of this kind. There are many areas of specialist design which are using computer graphics at the leading edge, but the message for the user in education is positive – the software is improving, the qualification being that we will all need phenomenally powerful computers to run this new stuff. Remember that in 1984, 256k memory was seen as more than most average people would ever need.

Hardware developments

Hardware presents the hard-pressed iT co-ordinator with a bewildering array of products designed to assist the designer or the artist. This is not the place to discuss the current ranges of each manufacturer, but it is worth noting one or two items that have appeared in recent years which would appear, from initial reports, to be making a real impact in classrooms; mention is also made of some of the newer technologies.

The range of input devices has generally remained fairly stable of late, as refinements become the order of the day – mice now come in all shape and sizes, they 'speak' along infrared beams to the processor, and they have shrunk to mere bumps on the surface of the laptop. Light pens still exist; keyboards are ergonomic; and now we have computers that will react to the voice of the user – the concept of drawing with one's voice is quite the most fascinating idea of all. Those of you in special education will remember MicroMike.

Traditionally, the mouse has held sway in the input field, complemented by the occasional use of a digitiser, video grabber or possibly a scanner. Graphics tablets too, have attracted a following, but only in the last 2 years or so have they become really attractive to the artist and designer. Two factors account for this – the gradual drop in cost, and the development of software that can really take full advantage of the more tactile nature of the tablet approach. Multimedia in itself does not provide revolutionary ideas for learning, but the peripheral hardware market is currently thriving. There are many inventive and imaginative approaches to combining a range of digital media: the by-product is a range of computers that will have increasing relevance to teachers already seeking to expand opportunities for learning. Hence, video grabbing, or capturing video clips from tape, and saving in digital format is now commonplace and cheap. The hardware to do this is now becoming part of the standard computer specification, as is sound recording; the possibilities for frame grabbing are therefore considerably enhanced.

Further progression from this process is to consider digital photography, an area of technology currently in a state of flux, although a worthy contender is the Canon Ion system, which stores images on tiny floppy discs, but which can be connected directly to a computer in order to view the photographs. The process is instant, hence the main advantage over CD-based storage, although space remains an issue. A quick browse through any of major computer magazines shows that the manufacturers' reaction to the problem is to specify larger and large hard disk systems.

The question of output, is more complex – for the typical school IT co-ordinator, wishing to develop an art and design facility, the range of options include:

Printing

• Monochrome:

    Laser: slow, high quality, expensive
    Inkjet: slow, good quality, cheaper than a laser
    Dot matrix: fast, low quality, cheap

• Colour:

    Thermal wax: slow, high quality, expensive
    Inkjet: slow, good quality, cheaper than thermal
    Dot matrix: faster than above, low quality
    Plotter: speed relative to complexity of image, high quality, expensive, specialist

Storage

• *Tape drive:* Good for backing up network, storage space limited only by number of tapes, reliable.

• *Floppy disk:* For personal use, storage space very limited for images, unreliable.

• *Internal hard drive:* Short-term back-up, space easily filled with images, reliable.

• *Removable hard drive:* Good back-up facility, no limitation to number of files, reliable.

• *Optical disk:* Good back-up facility, very reliable, fast access time

• *Floptical:* Reliable, fast access time, portable, inexpensive – could be the natural replacement of the floppy disk.

• *WORM drive:* Not really suitable for backing up, read/write CDs not yet viable, expensive, slow, long-term they will get better and could be the way to go.

Screens

- *Mono/colour:*   colour must be the way forward.
- *Resolution:*   24-bit colour is wonderful, but does not come cheap.
- *Size:*   The 14″ screen seems to be the standard, but any graphic work is much more effective on larger (19″, 20″ etc.) screens. There is a huge price difference.
- *Tube:*   Sony – expensive, high quality. Hitachi – cheaper, lower quality, but does it really matter?

There are numerous management implications here, including cost, but the administrator must decide at an early stage how a graphics system will be distributed. A simple paint package will run comfortably enough on a standard network of PC186 type machines, as shown in Case Study 1. The more advanced packages have more complex requirements, however. There is no prescriptive guide to successfully meeting graphics output demands: each scenario has its share of advantages and pitfalls. Printing is one area of particular difficulty. Students are keen to see the results of their labours, especially if colour output is an option, but the formula for deciding on a suitable environment is complex. Case Study 1 clearly shows one solution: a simple network with 3 network printers. Case Studies 2 and 3 offer an alternative: several open-access work areas with printers, with more suitable machinery within the subject-work area, albeit in smaller numbers.

We can also look forward to the growth in the use of Photo-CD in the educational field: despite the relative slowness of CDs as storage media, CD has been promoted as the next major breakthrough, on the basis of storage space, cost and universal appeal. Image collections have been available on CD for some time – the Hulton Deutsch Collection, for example – but the ability to transfer ordinary exposed camera film onto a digital format at the local branch of Boots, for a non-exorbitant sum, has exciting possibilities. Most CD players can now read this new format, and the image can be viewed, copied and pasted as normal. The cost of writing one's own CD is probably prohibitive at present but schools and colleges may seriously consider the purchase of a machine that will give them the option of designing, constructing and storing courseware on a CD, with the added attraction of the space to store images, sounds, video clips etc. We will then be able to enjoy the efforts of modern teacher-designed curriculum-based software, rather than some of the efforts that find their way into the educational market.

The case studies

The first Case Study is taken from the vocational and pre-vocational sector. The department featured appears well resourced but the hardware is mainly cast-offs from other departments, and software choices are limited. Fortunately, the department deals in training nursery nurses, who are likely to come across similar low-level machinery and software in their place of work.

Using Paintspa and Word for DOS, students were required to produce a simple glossary of terms used in their computer facility, with each item to be shown in diagrammatic form. The assignment clearly showed the requirements and levels of skill expected, by listing the features of each application which were to be used. This type of assignment is fairly typical of this level of BTEC work – 1st Award is aimed at early school leavers with relatively low grades at GCSE. It is predominantly skills based, but by including a number of common skills the project aims to encourage students' management and critical faculties.

Many of the BTEC students are disappointed to learn that IT is a fundamental part of all the BTEC courses, a feeling based possibly on negative experiences in school but also upon the perceived lack of relevance of IT to childcare. Nevertheless, the change in IT policy has proved successful, mainly due to the emphasis placed on the use of computers as an aid to learning, which is controlled by students. Open-access to learning is a feature of the course – facilities are available during normal working hours, and occasionally well into the evening. Good management of the network ensures that major problems are few. Files are stored on the network, with students retaining their own copies on floppy disk – regular 'clear-outs' of the network encourage students to manage their files efficiently.

This simple assignment encouraged students to see the system as an extra tool for their own use. Ownership is perhaps a key word here – at no time were students made to feel that the IT room was a 'special' or 'specialist' area, it is simply there to be used. It is used – lunch-time tends to see the room heavily populated. With this greater confidence in using the equipment, students will hopefully be able to develop their use of the facility as the course progresses and as they continue onwards to higher-level courses within the department, which approximately 90% will certainly do.

Student comments are revealing. All felt that Paintspa was eminently suitable for general 'design' tasks, but for more 'art-oriented' tasks, some degree of drawing skill was very helpful. The students had devised a number of ways to get round this problem, including the tracing of pictures onto OHP sheets – the sheets could then be attached to the VDU, and the image 'traced' on the screen, using a simple free-hand tool.

All the students appeared to have higher levels of perceived quality as a result of this assignment; students were very pleased with the result of the laser-printed word-processing. In terms of the image reproduction, many of them felt that a greater range of colour would have helped. One or two students were a little disappointed with the quality of the printed output, and on occasion, the sheer volume of images being processed led to paper jams and 'partial' printing. In addition, most felt that the time taken to print each picture was unacceptable. The colour printer was in use for much of the time, and the rapid turnover in ink cartridges meant that many of the printouts were of reduced quality. Some students had difficulty in remembering to select one of the three printer types and this caused mishaps in printing.

The second case study contrasts sharply with the above: the institution is a purpose-built example of an 'ideal' technology-based learning environment. The students, however, have the same needs as any others. The featured project, although differing in content, is another example of the importance of the computer as another tool that assists the user in achieving an end.

The project focuses on principles of design and does not emphasise IT skills. The Pneumatics course, part of the Technology curriculum, is based on the twin concepts of design and construction – students learn the theory of pneumatics circuits, practise designing them, then build the item using a range of suitable components. The use of IT substantially reduces the amount of time spent on laborious circuit drawing exercises, and Claris Works 2.0 has several features which have allowed the tutor to produce diagrams of exceptional quality: the gradient fills, as seen below, give an illusion of convexity that a standard 'pattern fill' cannot match.

In this study, the tutor has designed a 'bank' of component images using the drawing mode of Claris Works; this 'symbol library' is stored on a central machine in the Technology workshop, and students simply copy the libraries they require, along with a copy of the design brief onto their personal floppy disks, which they then take away and work on the component images. The retrieved image can be 'grouped', i.e. treated as one item, or 'ungrouped', i.e. reduced to constituent elements, such as lines, rectangles, etc. Figures 5.1 and 5.2 show a Single-Acting Cylinder. In ungrouped format the student is able to remove the cover of the cylinder to show the internal workings of the circuit.

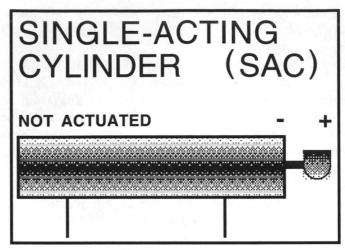

Figure 5.1 An example of the symbol library – a Single Acting Cylinder, shown covered

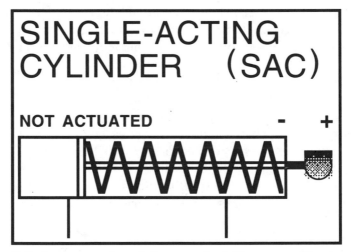

Figure 5.2 An example of the symbol library – Single Acting Cylinder, shown uncovered

The design brief lists the various components required to construct a circuit, and the student simply selects these items, uses the various drawing tools to connect up the circuit, then annotates the finished design to explain its workings. The design is completed by adding a shaded background, which by virtue of being an 'object', can be added at this stage of the design, and placed at the back of the design – again, background samples are supplied in the symbol library. At each stage, the students store copies of their work in progress on the tutor's machine, until they arrive at the finished article; at no stage is hard copy printed. Only when final assessment arrives is any hard proof required.

This method has proved very successful with both students and the teaching staff: savings in time are huge, student perceptions of their work is high and more time can be spent on practical work. The learning style is very flexible. The students generally split into two groups: one theory, one practical. At any one time, as the observation showed, students in the theory group could be anywhere in the building – the availability of common working areas, all featuring Claris Works, ensures that there is always somewhere to work. Students showed that they enjoyed the flexibility, and the trust shown in them and conveyed a sense of real pride in the results.

The scenario here raises some arguments as to the use of clip-art. This example describes some of the real advantages that creative use of IT can bring to classroom activities. There is a considerable amount of preparation time required, but the results justify the effort. Ultimately it is the tool idea that appears once again. Similar examples exist including a recent attempt to produce map-making symbols in Claris Works. A word here also for the software – there are a number of pneumatics modelling packages available, but the adaptation of a general-purpose application, familiar to users has ensured that extra investment is unnecessary. The latest version of Claris Works (2.0) was recently installed and has proved to have real benefits over the original, particularly with its advanced drawing features and painting tools, which allow the user to switch between the two styles of illustration. The word-processing and spreadsheet units are of a similar high quality. The greatest advantage of this application is its ability to combine seamlessly all the modules on the screen. The package is rapidly becoming the best-selling application on the Macintosh, and is making substantial inroads into the Windows market. Claris have also realised the value of educational support and have actively encouraged a wide free-flow and exchange of ideas, by assisting users to generate their own educational applications for free distribution in the educational community. These templates show the startling range of possibilities being used in primary through to secondary schools, across the whole curriculum.

In this study, the software has been used to great effect. In the long term, the tutors concerned with this project are also keen to take the concepts further; they are already talking to tutors dealing in electronics, with view to electrical circuit design, and are also investigating packages that will allow them to animate the diagrams, hence producing an entire design, build and test process on-screen, *before* building the real thing.

The third and final case study is 'art' oriented. The project is still in progress, but from the observations, several exciting developments in using computers within an art curriculum were discovered.

The project was an integrated examination of perspective – students started by looking at the mechanism by which drawings may be made using perspective tools, then followed up by making hand-drawn sketches of various interior views of the buildings. Using the example of Anthony Green, they were then able to take copied 'sections' of the drawing and produce a 'linked collage' effect. Running in parallel were a number of exercises based on colour, i.e. how colour shades and tints may be employed in enhancing the effects of perspective illustration. The computer input is treated very much as another complementary aspect of the project.

The flexible nature of this learning environment appears to work well – in art lessons, this approach would appear to be the most favoured, as at any one time, students could be engaged on a wide variety of activities, all based on the same project; the excellent level of resources is to be envied, but the resource is used constructively, and with great flair. Each student spends 6 weeks in his or her first term, in an induction course which gives them the basic skills to use Claris Works. Many of them will use only a part of the package, whilst others, as in this study, will be encouraged to explore and experiment with the features.

The software proved to be an excellent choice. As in the previous study, there are more specific packages on the market, including Letrastudio, which is ideally suited to distorting images, but the tutors and students were more comfortable with Claris Works, and it was able to do everything that was asked of it. A majority of the students displayed exceptional levels of skill in using the package, and were very familiar with the difference between 'draw'and 'paint' – they understood the advantages and disadvantages of each, and used their knowledge to full effect. The colour printouts cannot, unfortunately, be reproduced here, but are quite outstanding.

The learning appeared to be positive and enjoyable in an environment where the use of IT is second nature. The tools exist for students to cover a wide range of subject areas and interests, which they appear to have absorbed. In one or two cases, the art tutor was able to point out students of lower ability who appeared to have made much more progress than expected, purely as a result of having technology as an available alternative to a traditional approach; the concept of integrated emancipatory learning would appear to have an input here, and the overall impression is one of learners having the freedom to explore and making use of that freedom, on the basis that the tools for the job include technology, but that is all.

Final thoughts

Various curriculum guidance documents have been produced by the government, for the two areas of most concern: Art, and Design and Technology. These documents identify a model based on five major themes: handling information; communicating information; modelling; measurement and control; applications and effect. In Design and Technology, there are direct links to modelling, and control; more secondary linkages can be made to handling and communicating information. Both these strands feature prominently in Case Study 2. In the case of the Art curriculum, Case Study 3 clearly shows how the project has also followed suggested good practice. These include:

- Develop, organise and store ideas in visual form.
- Transfer a design from one medium to another.
- Reflect on how the use of IT has influenced the development of an image or design.

Yet in both cases, although these criteria are being met, IT in the school or college must be more than simply affixing activities and projects to simple statements of intent. As I have pointed out, IT must be a complementary process that crosses subject and skill areas, and if we are to ensure that this is the case, more resources need to be targeted at raising the awareness of teachers, Headteachers and IT Co-ordinators – not just in terms of IT skills but in teaching and learning. There are many examples of 'good practice' at the local level, but there appear to be few mechanisms for disseminating this good news nationally.

Art, and Design and Technology are areas where the 'doing' is an intrinsic part of the learning. Given the advantages of student-centred and resource-based learning, therefore, further issues are apparent. General resourcing levels are hugely variable: in Northamptonshire, the ratio of students to computers in the county's secondary schools varies enormously, as do the levels of hardware. Given the difficulties in deciding on 'new' equipment, as and when funds become available, the job of a school IT Co-ordinator becomes even less attractive, but the bottom line remains – better equipment and more of it . Project and assignment work is ideally suited to computer-based learning styles, but there is as much learning to be had, by the 'doing', as there is by achieving an objective. In other words, we must encourage the use of the computer to enhance the learning process, rather than to stress the product. From the artists' point of view, the message is even clearer:

72

open-ended work embodies diversity in interpretation, personal expression and creativity (Cooper, 1990).

Despite the pressures on time and resources, many Art and CDT teachers have taken IT on board. For the teacher, the need to provide a provocative and interesting range of stimuli to motivate and support students has always ensured that the quest for richer and more diverse resources, must continue. Nevertheless, it is clear that the use of computers cannot be seen in isolation; and few, if any, cases exist where straight IT lessons are taught on their own.

Case Study 1:

Computer Hardware
Keith Clark
Department of Care, Northampton College

Project Aims and Objectives

- To introduce students to the Nimbus PC186 network.
- To enable students to identify the different printers.
  (Laser/Star/Integrex) and the different printouts that can be obtained.
- To develop an understanding of the parts of the computer system.
- To identify the File Server and what activity it carries out.

To develop the following common skills that are required by the student to achieve the BTEC 1st Award:

- Manage own roles and responsibilities.
- Manage own time in achieving objectives.
- Undertake personal and career development.
- Transfer skills to new and changing situations and contexts.
- Present information in a variety of visual forms.
- Use a range of technological equipment and systems.

The Class/Students
17 students: 15 girls, 2 boys aged 16–17 years.
Most have very few qualifications with poor grades at GCSE.

Software	Hardware
Paintspa, SPA Associates Ltd	24 Nimbus PC186 CPUs, with 12" colour monitors; RM Z-Net network
Stand-alone: £36.00 Network/16 user: £99.00 Pixel-based colour paint program	Integrex Colourjet 132; Brother HP-4 Postscript Laser Printer

Project Description

Organisation
This was a 5-week assignment to prepare a glossary of terms currently used in describing computer hardware. Product took the form of a word-processed booklet describing, explaining and depicting each particular item. An assessment guide gave a clear outline of the necessary skills to be used in achieving the various attainment levels.

* Group introduced to the different parts of the computer system, their names and their purpose.
* Group introduced to the Paintspa package and the facilities/ operations you can do with it.
* Group introduced to the assessment paper and the assessment criteria.
* Over a period of time (stated on the Assessment Paper) candidates organise the way of completing the paper.

The environment is a relatively inflexible format: a 24-station computer suite. The room has been arranged to facilitate networking, i.e. machines must have access to power and networking points. Furniture (computer desks with cabling troughs) is arranged to allow the maximum number of machines to be used at any one time.

Outcomes
Students learnt about the computer hardware and the purpose of it. I questioned them, I listened to them talking between each other. I observed them drawing the particular piece of hardware. In marking the final completed assignment, I further questioned them to make sure they had achieved the objectives.

Assessment included general discussions with the group in order to ascertain their opinion of the assignment. In general, the students felt much more comfortable with the network, and could clearly pick out each of the various items and describe its purpose and function; they all agreed that they could demonstrate and explain the package to others. Many of the students had experienced Paintspa at school, but felt that they were now much more competent in using all of its tools – several students mentioned that it was particularly suitable for younger children.

Did things go according to plan?
* Organisational problems included the long print queue – about 5

minutes for each printout!
- No automatic feed out on the Integrex: manual feed very time consuming!
- Choosing the wrong printer selection caused hassle.
- Some students with strong artistic abilities spent a lot of time on pictures which caused time pressure at the end of the course.
- Conceptual problems: I feel some students are still confused on the various items. Student feedback required.

Future development
Still to decide on this after marking the assignments and talking to students.

Case Study 2:

CAD Pneumatics
Mark Rogers
Brooke Weston City Technology College

Project Aims and Objectives
To promote an understanding of the nature of pneumatic circuits. Students will gain experience in drawing pneumatic circuits using CAD facilities, as well as manufacturing testing and evaluating circuits.

The Class/Students
Year 8; 20 students per group;mixed ability; even gender split and all other factors very mixed.

Software	Hardware
Claris Works 2.0, Claris stand-alone: £90.00 net licence negotiable	Apple Macintosh LCII with 14" colour monitor
Fully integrated package, featuring Word Processor, Spreadsheet, Database, Communications, Paint & Draw	Apple Macintosh IIci with 16" colour monitor
	1 machine to 2 students

Project Description

Organisation
The project is based on a 5-week programme of study, including a general introduction to pneumatics and investigations into safety, circuit diagrams, single and double-acting cylinders with 3 and 5 port valves, circuit diagram design and construction, culminating in a differentiated

design brief.

The design briefs cater for mixed-ability students – an example of the Extended Level Brief concerns the design and operation of a sliding door. The brief requires the student '... to design a device that will open and close the door in a safe and efficient manner. The device must not move until operated by a valve. Neither must it return automatically.'

The course is split evenly between practical and design exercises, the latter being based on the use of a 'symbol library' provided by the tutor and available on the hard disks of the computers in the room. Students open the library (see example) and select the items as required. They are then able to construct the circuit using a 'Brief Format' – a guide to laying out the finished article, which gives notes on adjusting and anno-tating the final presentation. On completion, the design is stored on the students' floppy disk and the tutor's hard disk; printing is not called upon until the presentation of all coursework for GCSE assessment.

Organisation of the environment is flexible because students may go elsewhere in the college to find a computer. The group is divided into two sub-groups – one practical and one that completes the graphics documentation, e.g. circuit diagrams.

Outcomes

The students learnt to understand pneumatics applications, by the correct constitution and recording of the pneumatics circuits. Software was a major factor in motivating the students; the students respond well to the images they can create. As the subject was a new area for the majority of the students, the novelty of it appeared to arouse motivation. The style of learning led to a positive response from the students – the high expectations placed on them and the flexible learning environment certainly contributed to a productive working atmosphere.

Did things go according to plan?

In general, yes. The students' aims and objectives were made very clear right from the start, as each pupil is given a copy of the programme of study, at the beginning of the term. There were few organisational or technical problems; all the students are very computer literate, and the ease of use and intuitive nature of the application ensures that major problems occur rarely. Ideally we need to include an improved ratio of machines to students, i.e. 1:1.

Future Development

The experience will definitely be repeated, but in development terms the

76

symbol library will need to be updated and expanded. A logical progression will be to introduce animation into the graphic work, allowing students to design, model and test the circuit on-screen, prior to physical construction.

Case Study 3:

New Perspectives
Lesley O'Callaghan
Brooke Weston City Technology College

Project Aims and Objectives
The aims of the computer application element of this project were as follows:

• To enable the students to become familiar with a range of skills associated with the production of computer images, which will be of value outside the scope of this particular project.
• To raise the students' awareness and appreciation of using the computer as a powerful tool for the creation of images.
• To enable students to produce higher quality one-point perspective images than they may have been able to produce using traditional means.
• To enable students to combine and distort views in a way that they have found difficult using any other methods.

The Class/Students
21 students: Year 9, with even gender split, of mixed ability.

Software	Hardware
Claris Works 2.0, Claris stand-alone: £90.00 net licence negotiable	Apple Macintosh LCII with 14" colour monitor
Fully integrated package, featuring Word Processor, Spreadsheet, Database, Communications, Paint & Draw	Apple Macintosh IIci with 16" colour monitor
	5 machines in total
Letrastudio 2.0, Letraset stand-alone: £200.00	2 Apple Colour Scanners with Ofoto software
Powerful Type and line-art manipulation package.	2 Apple Colour Printers

Project Description

Organisation
The computer application element was part of a more extensive project on one- and two-point perspective which included the use of traditional

techniques. As the projéct progressed, all students were introduced to the work of a practising artist, Anthony Green. Green uses unusual and distorted views of interiors in his work. At this stage, students who opted to extend their work using the computer package can further develop their ideas using both the original application and a new, more powerful package.

Although on occasions, technical support was available, it was more usual for the teacher to manage the class.

The art suite has five machines, two scanners and two colour printers. Other machines are available at other locations throughout the college, but as most students required teacher support and input they were not used. The organisation within this learning environment provided the students with the opportunity to view other students work on the computer which then provides a stimulus for further developments.

Outcomes
Students who participated in this element of the project now possess higher level of skills and applications of techniques using the computer package. Towards the end of the project, it became evident that students were now able to produce more sophisticated drawings with a lower level of teacher support. Although there is no objective evidence available, it is my view that the students have raised or reinforced their appreciation/awareness of the possibilities that a computer package offers. The combination of the computer element and the traditional method has resulted in students becoming aware of the use of one-point perspective to create the illusion of depth, in a composition. Although not all students found it easy to produce this effect, they were all able to evaluate their output realistically. Students were pleased with the high quality of their final product in the one-point perspective work.

Some students were attracted to the computer for negative reasons: avoidance of the more traditional methods, possibly due to a conviction that the computer-aided work will require less effort. Similarly, more able students sometimes avoided using the computer which they felt de-skilled them.

Did things go according to plan?
There were no major conceptual problems because of the amount of groundwork covered in the early stages.

At the start of the project, Claris Works was only available on a limited number of machines; although all students had a short introduction to the possibilities of using the package, their hands-on experience had to be spread over many lessons. This would therefore always run alongside other activities related to the programme of study: objective drawing of the college environment, colour theory and application, and developing painting skills. Now that Claris Works is available on most machines, it would be possible to book enough machines for the whole class to use, and therefore possible to cover this aspect of the project over two lessons: introducing the students to the package allowing experimentation; and acquisition of the necessary skills to produce an image in perspective. Further developments with distorting the image could still be offered as a possibility to run alongside other activities.

One major problem was storage to floppy disk; many students found that when they returned to their work, an error had occurred on their disk, and consequently their work was lost. A disheartening experience. At present I am storing all students work on disks of higher quality and have not experienced any problems to date, although this does mean having enough disks to accommodate all relevant work.

On occasions, the internal memory of the machine was not large enough to carry out certain operations – in particular, the selection and duplication of large areas of the image. This is when technical support is invaluable!

Future Developments
Developments include the refining of the existing project into a package which students can use more independently, by providing a variety of support materials which reduce the need for extensive teacher intervention. Also, the further exploration of the possibilities of distortion with a view to producing more complex images that form the basis of both two- and three-dimensional development.

Chapter 6
Databases

Jean Underwood
with Doug Dickinson, Kath Lee and Owen Lynch

Education and information-handling skills

Four years ago we considered that there were compelling arguments for using information-handling packages in schools (Underwood and Underwood, 1990). We argued that information-handling packages were an enabling technology which were seen by many as one of the most effective ways of using computers in school, for three reasons. Firstly because the software exploits the full potential of the machine itself – as in the adult world, information processing by computer allows rapid and increasingly complex manipulations of data. Secondly, it offers the opportunity for children to collate and interrogate their own material from the environment and form their own mental reconstructions of the world as they understand it. Thirdly, the use of databases can lead to a reduction in inauthentic labour, that is work which is not intrinsically valued as part of the learning experience. Learners often spend far more time on tasks such as completing simple computations or conducting frequency counts, rather than thinking about the relationships within the data. This places severe limits on the amount of data that can be manipulated, and downgrades the activity from being an example of real-world research problem solving to yet another classroom exercise. Students actively involved in collecting and organising data not only have ownership of the data, because they have collected it, but they are also able to use large bodies of data because of the emancipation provided by the processing power of the computer.

The premise on which I have argued for the use of databases in schools is that thinking skills are actively encouraged by the use of data storage and retrieval systems. Information retrieval packages will have an impact on classificatory skills (Underwood, 1986), and many teachers are using such programs with this educational goal specifically in mind (Underwood and Underwood, 1987). Additionally, in quizzing a database even young children can begin to ask 'good' questions and be introduced to a hypothesis-testing-strategy approach to learning.

These are heady claims, but is there any evidence that our predictions have any basis in classroom practice today? The aim of this chapter is to reflect further on the educational benefits which we predicted would accrue when children and students use database packages. I have drawn on the classroom experiences of several colleagues to illustrate the varied and effective use of databases in schools. A synopsis of their experiences is presented in the three case studies at the end of this chapter.

Before further discussion of the evidence for our claims of educational benefits I feel it would be useful to look at the way in which database software has developed over the last 5 years. For the changes in the software have not only had a profound effect on classroom practice, I suggest that they have brought about significant changes in the learning opportunities available to children. This is a point that I shall return to after the following review of some current software.

A database is a database or is it?

What is a database? Databases are organisational structures into which information is placed and from which the information can be retrieved and represented. The nature of that organisational structure and the method of data retrieval are two key ways in which databases differ one from another. These differing characteristics can have profound impacts on the ease of use of the program and on the cognitive experiences presented to the learner using them. The organisational structure underpinning early educational databases took the form of either a hierarchy or a binary-tree (SEEK), or tabular–matrix (GRASS, KEY, PINPOINT and FILEMAKER Pro). The use of network structures with their pathways and common links and nodes were less extensively used in educational systems but these now underpin many of the hypertext based information systems. Network structures allow multiple pathways through the data with all the freedom to get lost that implies!

Educational database packages have changed dramatically over the last 5 years. At the end of the 1980s databases were unglamorous but useful tools helping us to organise and retrieve information. But technological developments have revolutionised this humble tool and databases now consist of not just text but images, sound and video, with the result that it is increasingly difficult to say what constitutes a database. In this section I should like to illustrate, through examples, the nature of the changes in the databases before going on to consider the impact of those changes on children's and students' learning.

JUNIOR PINPOINT and PINPOINT (Longman Logotron) are typical examples of the new database tool. As for most new software they are icon driven and employ point and click technology which makes them easier to use than the old command line databases such as INFORM (see Underwood and Underwood, 1990). A key focus of development for such packages has been in the graphical presentation of retrieved data. Whereas the graphing facility of INFORM was restricted to a simple histogram, PINPOINT provides a range of graphs and charts. Students are particularly attracted to the three-dimensional pie chart! The graphing facilities are also integrated into the package. New users may be saying but of course I can move effortlessly from retrieving my data to graphing it, such facilities have long been available in old stalwarts such as GRASS (Newman Software). This was not true for programs such as OURFACTS, one of the most commonly used programs in primary schools. Here the result of a search could not be graphed. The graphing facilities were totally separate from the search and sort facilities, and to move from one to another required the user to exit from the database and reload the data file.

The PINPOINT programs also allow the user to import pictures into the data templates. The ability to move text and, in some cases, image data into and out of the database from other packages, as in this case, or between the elements of an integrated package as in DATASWEET (Kudlian Soft) is now an accepted norm for new databases. DATASWEET is an information handling and presentation package in five parts, incorporating database, spreadsheet and graphing facilities, but the emphasis is on the database software. Each part works well but movement between the individual programs is clumsy. Many teachers, such as Owen Lynch (Case Study 3) use only two or three parts of the overall program. EXCEL (Microsoft) is the world leader in spreadsheets but it also incorporates database and graphing facilities (see Chapter 7). The focal point of CLARIS WORKS is the word processor but it too is an integrated package containing word processor, graphics, spreadsheet and database tools (see Chapter 5). It is at this point that we start to ask what do we mean by database software? Secondly, is this integration of tools all benefit with no costs?

The Mapper Series (TAG) highlights another shift in the nature of educational databases. This is a family of programs each of which covers a typical primary school topic area. Currently there are three members of the family: BODYMAPPER, WEATHERMAPPER, and HOMEMAPPER. The latter is particularly liked by the teachers I have worked with on INSET courses.

In what ways is this software different from other information handling packages? In the first instance the packages are not sold as databases, rather they are topic based software, each supported by a curriculum information pack. If we look at BODYMAPPER, the first and least ambitious of the programs, we find that the database element is only a part of the software. This program supports the familiar topic 'Ourselves', just as the early version of OURFACTS did and does. The use of images and diagrams alongside text to represent the information held in the file is a key feature of this program (Figure 6.1).

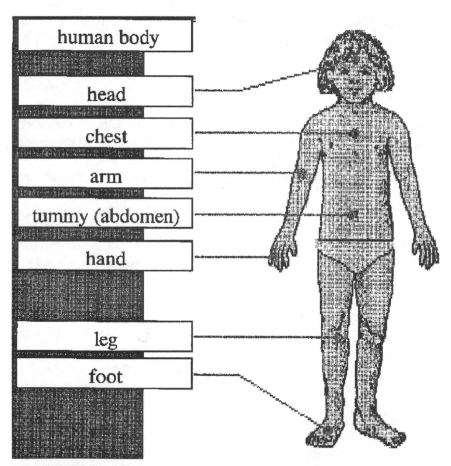

Figure 6.1 A typical BODYMAPPER screen

The use of images to support the children's understanding of themselves has gone down well with the staff and children I have worked with. A number have commented favourably on the sensitivity of the software to issues of equality. It will generate images of children of various ethnic groups, and the teacher can decide whether bodies will appear clothed or unclothed in response to the cultural background of their children. All this, of course, is at a cost – this program is memory hungry. When it first appeared the Archimedes version required 2 Megabytes of working memory but the standard machine on sale to primary schools was half this and additional memory for Acorn machines was particularly expensive at that time. In addition the program is not cheap and fulfils a very specific area of the curriculum rather than being a general tool supporting a range of topics.

As far as the development of information-handling skills are concerned the most significant difference between this software and say OURFACTS is that there is a ready-made data structure into which the children enter their own measurements.

A further example of this personalisation of a curriculum package can be found in the excellent package BATTLE OF THE SOMME. Here a laser disk, plus accompanying software, provides a wealth of material in text, image, sound and video clips on the First World War and in particular on the Somme campaign. Included in the package are the details of a one particular regiment heavily involved in the fighting. This data file can be changed and the students working with package can enter data for a regiment from their home locality.

We can see then a trend from open tools devoid of data and data structures to pre-designed shells into which children enter their measurements. We move from here of course to those packages which provide both the structure and the data. While it has been possible to buy sets of data for a wide range of databases, for example the excellent files which can be purchased alongside the KEY database, this move to providing a structured resource which the user interrogates has become of particular significance with the development of cheap CD-ROM technology. Commerce and industry has for some years had access to large data sets through main-frame computers but the difficulties of gaining access to this technology and the expense of becoming a member of one of these information clubs prohibited all but the most ambitious institutions from joining the game. CD-ROM is changing all that. As this book is published an estimated two thousand primary schools in England and Wales will be receiving their CD players and disks under the recently announced Department for Education initiative. Many, but perhaps not all, of those disks will contain large data sets designed to support resource-based learning.

Not all such resources are on CD-ROM, of course. MacGLOBE and PcGLOBE (Brøderbund) run on low-power PCs and Macs. This

84

program is essentially a simple electronic atlas and world database which can be used to support a wide range of subject areas and age ranges. Figure 6.2 is a typical map and Figures 6.3 shows that the range of data encompasses more than standard import and export figures.

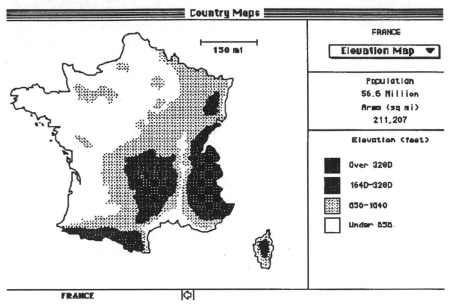

Figure 6.2 Relief Map of France from MacGlobe, © 1992, Brøderbund Software, Inc. All Rights Reserved. Used by permission.

The ability to make comparisons between chosen countries across specific topics is very useful as is shown by this comparison of Primary Student to Teacher ratios in the European Union. Secondary colleagues may ask why I have only include the primary comparison. The UK figures for secondary student:teacher ratios are very much in line with countries such as France and Germany; it is primary schools that operate at a disadvantage. Careful selection of data to make your point is of course a key part of data-handling skills!

The problem of what is a database becomes even more perplexing when discussing CD-ROMs. Is the CRUCIBLE CD-ROM a database or not? This features an electronic learning resource centred around Arthur Miller's play of that name, and includes the text of the play, interviews with actors, programmes notes and excerpts from the play.

Typical CD-ROMS available to schools include encyclopaedias of which GROLIER is generally seen to be one of the best. BRITISH BIRDS (the British Library) is described as a nature reference package.

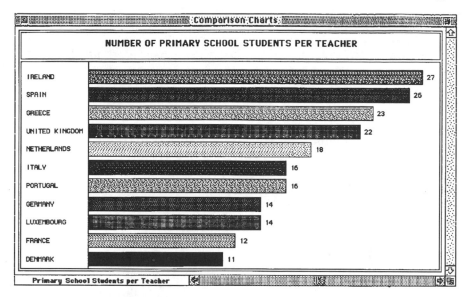

Figure 6.3 Comparison of primary student:teacher ratios for European Community MacGlobe, © 1992, Brøderbund Software, Inc. All Rights Reserved. Used by permission.

This encyclopaedia of birds contains a file of key data plus maps and images. Additional features include the tutorial package, curriculum guide and quiz. This particular package for Acorn machines can use older monitors but increasingly these multi-media databases require multi-synch monitors. Colour of course is a necessity for many packages.

Text-based ROMS are less demanding on hardware and can be very useful. Typical of these is the TIMES & SUNDAY TIMES CD-ROM which contains a year's worth of 'news' articles. Searching is by keyword within the title of an article or the body of the text. Other national newspapers from home and abroad, for example the Scottish HERALD and Le MONDE, are also available. The potential of these text-based resources is enormous. Research into topics such as desertification and child abuse can be supported by these packages. And of course there is a wealth of material for the media studies group and for the modern linguists. How about the view of Britain from Paris?

To sum up, database software is increasingly likely to:

• Be part of a suite of programs including graphing and charting facilities, spreadsheet functions and some level of word processing.
• Employ menus or icons as the means of moving around the database.
• Use keyword and Boolean searching as well as full sort facilities.

- Use images as well as text to produce a more friendly feel to the database.
- Require significantly more disk storage space and working memory (RAM) to be operate efficiently.
- Require the new breed of multi-synch monitors.

Also there is an accelerating tendency to:

- Move away from the providing just the database tool to more specific software either in the form of ready structured files to receive student data or reference files of data to be consulted.
- Use CD-ROMs as the storage medium.

The case for database use in the classroom

I have written elsewhere, and in some detail, about the research evidence supporting the assertion that there are very real benefits of using information-handling packages in primary and secondary classrooms (Underwood and Underwood, 1990). In that discussion I put forward the argument that databases were particularly useful in stimulating a process-oriented education through the support of problem-solving activities. Further supportive evidence of the value of information-handling packages to children's thinking is documented in Brown and Howlett (1994). There is insufficient space to re-argue the case here but I would like to briefly re-state in what ways use of these tools can be beneficial.

Essentially the arguments for the educational use of databases are that they:

- Stimulate classificatory ability, an underpinning cognitive skill all learners need to develop, through a developing understanding of similarities and differences and of category boundaries.
- Facilitate multiple representations of data, for example taking numerical data as a line graph, thus aiding the learner's understanding of those data.
- Facilitate the comparison of data through scatter graphs or comparison charts, thus aiding the learner's understanding of those data.
- Facilitate the manipulation of large data sets both de-trivialising the research activity and opening up opportunities for asking better questions.
- Encourage skills of selection of data and of modes of representing that data.

- Encourage the development of questioning skills.
- Encourage an understanding of the scientific method and the development of hypothesis-testing skills.

The conditions under which data handling activities are likely to be effective include:

- The activity is clearly defined, purposeful and also meaningful in the learner's eyes.
- The learner has developed a mental map of the database that is the structure of the file is transparent to the user.
- Graphing tools provide meaningful representations of the data

**Opportunities for learning:
Three classroom experiences and more**

In 1990 I presented a series of experimental studies and case studies to support the claims I am making here but since then educational data-bases have gone through a significant period of development. What has been the impact of these readily visible changes to database software on the type of educational activities that are now taking place in class-rooms? If, as I am arguing, there has been a shift in the nature of class-room use of databases has this also changed the nature of the learning opportunities? Of course the case I am presenting, and will now expand upon, is that the move from open tool to shell to filled filing cabinet has shifted the emphasis away from the development of classificatory skills to information-retrieval and information selection skills. The three case studies presented at the end of this chapter are illustrative of the changes within educational use of databases.

Starting from scratch
I have spent some time arguing the case for classificatory activities in the classroom. What children need is a purpose for classifying before they go onto the arduous, but potentially rewarding, task of creating a data file. The act of building a data file should require children to set goals or pose a problem, collect and select data, and to organise those data in such away that the initial question can be resolved or refined (Case Study 3). Each of these activities presents opportunities for exciting learning outcomes but this is an example of the whole being very definitely more than the sum of its parts. Good research questions are an aid to the definition of relevant data and suggest best-fit solutions for data organisation. In Underwood and Underwood (1990) we detailed the careful steps to success taken by a class of 8 year olds investigating the important issue of road safety around their school. In

Case Study 3 (Birds of the Ennerdale Valley), our young ornithologists offer another excellent example of the database being used as a tool to support research activities. Indeed it is this central goal of developing a climate in which good research can take place which is at the heart of the project.

In the Road Safety project the children conducted a detailed survey of environmental features and road traffic which they felt aided or hindered pedestrian road safety. The children found that the way in which they had structured their file prevented them accessing the data in a meaningful way, yet they knew the data was in the file. After all, they had put it there! A knowledge of what was in the file gave these children the confidence to ask why they could not retrieve the required data. They came to the conclusion that the structure of the file was upside down. This then led the children to restructure their file and to enter data into place-name records with road-safety features defining fields which then allowed them to identify localities with cumulative high safety risk factors such as heavy lorry traffic and poor pedestrian visibility. Transposition of data in this way is a highly skilled activity. Should we be surprised that the children succeeded? The key to this achievement lay in the nature of the problem. Crossing the road had meaning for these children, they knew what the goal was and it was within their power to manipulate the material into an appropriate form.

Among practitioners at all levels Papert's (1980) 'continuity principle' is readily accepted. The premise is that the learner's cognitive performance will improve over a wide range of measures, if the educational experience build's upon the learner's own experiences. As for the Road Safety project, Owen Lynch uses this argument when explaining why his young ornithologists happily sustained a project over 15 months with what might appear to be numerous set-backs, and without producing clear definitive answers to their initial questions at the end of the project. In a third investigation by secondary-school pupils of their own dental health a key outcome of the study was the way in which children re-formulated questions following output from the database. For example, the children felt that brushing teeth twice a day would lead to an improvement in health, that is fewer fillings, extractions and bleeding gums. They were surprised to find that the evidence did not support this hypothesis, but still felt that their initial assumption was valid. The hypothesis was therefore modified to explore the effects of not two but one cleaning per day. This was correlated to dental health.

In all three of these studies the students had started from a clear research agenda and framework which drove their field survey and controlled the database structure. A significant element of the Ennerdale

Study is the level of responsibility placed on the children not only to collect and organise their data but to provide their own quality control to maintain the integrity of the database. Their willingness and acceptance of the need to cross-check the reliability and validity of their data sources is breathtaking. I wonder if my doctoral students are being as rigorous?

Here then we can see that the children are achieving many of the learning outcomes I have listed above. They asked good questions, they classified the data, they interrogated the file and revised their thinking in the light of the information retrieved. All in all they are very satisfactory experiences. Is it always like this? Were there no problems? I would strongly suggest that this type of work does not succeed unless the children have a genuine and personal interest in the data – ownership is very important. 'Doing databases' for the sake of using the tool without a clearly defined purpose generally leads to poor learning outcomes. The tool needs to be embedded meaningfully in the curriculum.

Also there were problems but on the whole the children thought them through and produced workable solutions. The problem of the graphing facilities in the Ennerdale study could not be resolved, however. Interpreting graphs is no easy matter at the best of times but when there are bugs in the program, or the graphing algorithm is suspect, then machines will return nonsense which can confuse the learners. A key role for teachers in educational database use is checking the validity of the output from graphing and charting utilities.

Using a shell
What then are the educational advantages of using already structured database shell such as BODYMAPPER or THE FIVE STAR AWARDS SCHEME software? Obviously many of the key questions about how to structure and code the data being collected are taken away from the users so one would not expect this sought of activity to support the development of classificatory skills development. There is still a sense of ownership of the data, however, as Doug Dickinson (Case Study 1) has shown. He again emphasises the children's role in maintaining quality control and he confirms that the children were keen to check their own and other pupils' data because the output, a statement of their performance, was meaningful to them.

A second important reason for using this shell software is ease and speed of getting projects off the ground. The initial framework of the project is provided. This makes such programs extremely useful as introductions to information handling because there is a 'guarantee' of successful outcomes. Indeed such packages can provide excellent training packages for both the teacher and the learner before choosing to use a full database tool. Owen Lynch emphasises in the Ennerdale study the need for pre-training before embarking on as ambitious a project as he presents here. Also the use of such packages with primary age children meets Keystage 1 and 2 National Curriculum objectives to retrieve information and to enter information into a database.

Other people's data
Are we still building a world of information or are we manipulating a pre-digested world? Does the answer to this question matter?

The quality of query formulation is the key to the effective questioning of a database. There are two problems here. The first is to get the learner to ask a worthwhile question, and this is no small matter. The second problem lies in translating the question into the query syntax of the specific database being used. Thus the learner needs to be clear about the goal of the search – what information will provide an answer to the enquiry – and also clear about how to ask the computer to provide that information in an intelligible form. The very method of constructing and interrogating computer databases requires a clear understanding of that structure. It is more difficult to fulfil this need for a mental map of the data structure when using pre-constructed data sets.

Although the problem of understanding the structure of the data for ready-made files is still with us, a second problem, defining a search, seems to be less difficult with the newer software. Learners are far less likely to have to deal with the complexity of transposing natural language questions into query language, rather they will use menu selections or keyword searches. Many databases now operate on the simple keyword search mechanism, in which the data file is scanned for all the occurrences of the specified word, for example for the term the *desertification* in the TIMES CD-ROM. Students need to possess considerable skills of identification of the areas they will want to investigate. Keyword searches can act as a trigger for ideas not already thought of and sometimes act as memory joggers. Searches are usually refined through the use of Boolean Logic. This is not a simple matter: an understanding of the concepts of and/or searches is required to enable students to use the technology effectively.

There are cognitive benefits from using query procedures as it requires students to understand the process of electronic retrieval of information. The quality of the searching is an indication of the student's own power to both understand and manipulate data. One of the sixth formers in Kath Lee's school (Case Study 2) provides an illustration of the need to understand the material being searched and to have a clearly defined question or goal at the onset of the search. A student, using the GROLIER Encyclopaedia CD-ROM, was searching for information regarding human embryology and genetics. Her first search using 'genetics' gave her far too many references. Before continuing, the student was asked to consider what she wanted information about and to reformulate her question on the basis of those reflections. She subsequently refined her search to 'genetic engineering' and 'human' and 'embryology' and was successful in her query. Similarly, a group of students using the TIMES CD-ROM, required information about recent natural disasters and typed in 'Natural Disaster' as a single term but found no references. However, choosing 'disasters' and 'natural' provided the information they required.

The majority of the sixth-form students in Case Study 2 were only trained to use the ECCTIS CD-ROM, nevertheless they were able to transfer their information retrieval skills to other CD-ROMs even though there was no coherence in the interrogation software. It was found that a high percentage of the students in Year 12 (66%) were confidently using CD-ROM for specific tasks in a variety of curriculum areas. Kath Lee argues that different search mechanisms forced her students to develop different strategies, which can only encourage them to be adaptable and enhance their understanding of the concept of retrieval. These students were very enthusiastic about the ease and speed with which they could gain information, the ability to progress along lines of personal enquiry and the flexibility to take relevant information away. Indeed access to CD-ROM actively supported independent approaches to learning and prompted a very enthusiastic response, for example two students spent a full day at the workstation consolidating their skills and refining their searches. She questions whether they would have shown the same dedication if they had been using a paper-based resource. She also noted that her students accessed CD-ROM just 'to have a look', out of 'general interest' and 'to find out what this media can do' and not always in direct response to specific studies.

Evaluating the output of a search
At a recent NCET meeting I listened to what some might consider to be an apocryphal tale. This concerned the student who had collated from electronic sources an impressive file on the Trojan War, but who, in response to his teacher's casual remark 'It was a strange horse, wasn't it?', replied 'What Horse?'. There is a real concern here. Are our students working with information or simply collecting it?

92

Students need to be able to develop their evaluative powers to determine what information is relevant and useful. Although students are able to use their new-found skills to download extracts of Shakespeare or global news report and incorporate them into their essays, in what way are they making that information their own. They need not only to make careful selection of retrieved data but also to integrate that data into a new whole as a response to the question they have selected to answer. We need to teach our students how to use primary and secondary resource material. Information-handling skills, as any librarian will tell you, need careful nurturing. Not the least of these skills is the need to question the authority of the data source, as in Case Study 3.

Plagiarism and wholesale copying of information is not a new problem in education but it has become acute following the widespread introduction of information technologies. Many students incorporate far too much inappropriate material into their work. Students must develop a higher level of information sifting. There are practical considerations as well as moral and learning issues here. As Kath Lee points out if a student decides to print out all articles rather that selected extracts, it affects the performance of the computer network and causes some disquiet from other users, not to mention the number of wasted sheets of paper and printer ribbon.

Summary

The developments in database software are beginning to have profound effects on information handling within our schools and colleges. The case studies which have been described here have been presented as demonstrations of the learning gains which can be made when children work with databases. The current move towards shells and towards ready-made data stores has had two key effects. The first is that for many teachers and students there is now a much easier entry point to database use than was previously the case. Secondly, the shift in emphasis from structuring of information to that of information selection and retrieval requires us to teach students actively how to use and evaluate primary and secondary data stores.

Case Study 1:

Monitoring Athletic Progress
Doug Dickinson
Orchard Primary School, Castle Donington, Leicestershire

Project Aims and Objectives:
The principal aims were to:

- present athletics to a wider school audience
and
- motivate the children.

In addition I wanted to:

- extend the use of IT across the curriculum by using a database package for a 'real' purpose.

The Class/Students
Sixty children aged 9–10 years were involved in the project. This was a mixed ability and gender group.

Software	Hardware
The Five Star Awards Scheme	Archimedes
October Pen	IBM compatibles
Little Hayden Lane	Research Machines
Clanfield	
Hampshire	
£20.00	
3.5" floppy	

Project Description

Organisation
The software is an administrative database that handles athletics performance scores which it relates to a carefully calculated points scale. Children measured their own performance on the athletics field and then accessed the database to record that performance. The children kept a hard copy of their performance data on a record card. This data was then entered onto the database at times convenient to the pupil, the class as a whole and the class teacher. There were queuing problems at peak demand times just after athletics practice.

Outcomes
The children quickly learnt how to access and interrogate this pre-built data structure. They were able to monitor their own performances, amend the data and they also learnt to check the accuracy of the entered data.

The children 'owned' the data that they had entered, it meant something to them personally and they wanted an accurate printout of their performance. They were highly motivated to work in this way.

Did things go according to plan?:
The simple answer is yes. The software is very robust – no-one managed to crash it! Hardware shortages were the main problem. We only had two machines available to the 60 pupils, and these machines were also used for other work.

Future Developments
The project is to be repeated next year, and we expect to continue building up this record of performance over subsequent years. A new version of the software due out in 1994 promises to be easier to use as it reduces the number of screens the children have to work with. Both the efficiency of the data recording and the immediacy and sense of ownership of the data would be improved if we had a portable computer available at the side of the athletics track. This would reduce the queuing back in the classroom and the need for paper records.

We could make use of the aggregated data in the future.

Case Study 2:

CD-ROM in the Sixth Form
Kath Lee
King Edward VII, Melton Mowbray, Leicestershire

Project Aims and Objectives
To introduce staff and students to the use of CD-ROM and demonstrate its advantages, and subsequently to give all students access to electronic retrieval facilities.

As part of the NCET pilot a CD-ROM station was supplied and placed within the sixth form and made available to Year 12 students, their tutors and teachers. The decision to base the CD-ROM facilities within the sixth form was made for a number of reasons:

- To support a new school initiative to promote independent learning currently undertaken within the 16–19 phase.
- To target a manageable number of staff with the belief that feedback would encourage all staff to want to become involved.
- A positive decision to capitalise on the demand from students for Higher Education information supplied via the ECCTIS CD-ROM. It was envisaged that this would ensure that students developed transferable skills, self-confidence and at the same time promote their ability to work independently.

The Class/Students
180 Year 12 students.

Software	Hardware
ECCTIS CD-ROM	RM 386 M Series CD-ROM
NB: This is a text-based ROM with low hardware needs. Multimedia ROMS are more demanding	Standalone and networked machines including RM 186 (under IBM emulation), AX, M series and S series

Don't Panic: for the more technically minded

The CD-ROMs in use at King Edward VII fall broadly into three categories:

- DOS applications
- Windows applications
- Multimedia applications

All of these are installed on stand-alone workstations in the Independent Learning Centres and are launched from a 'Windows' (version 3.0 or 3.1) menu, the multimedia applications making use of 'sound blaster' cards in these machines. In terms of networking, a number of titles are made available to students using two different systems. The main school network runs RM Net 3.1 on 386 VX servers with a 386 M Series CD-ROM server running Optinet version 1.30 linked to three external CD-ROM drives on a single card. The CD-ROMs are made available to users in their own personal area using Research Machine's 'Micro Menu' program which maximises the amount of memory available in a workstation whilst attached to the network, though of course this varies with station type (a mixture of PC186, AX, M series and S series). Most recently released CD-ROM titles require the use of VGA graphics or better and so only text-based CD-ROMs run on the older PC186's under IBM emulation.

The sixth-form network runs RM NetLM version 1.01g on a 486 Systembase file server with a 486 S series CD-ROM server running Optinet version 2.00c linked also to three external CD-ROM drives on a single card. The user environment is currently Windows 3.0 and network stations are all S series 386 and above. Station memory availability is particularly critical though we have had no major problems in running similar titles to the main school network.

A multimedia CD-ROM title has been successfully installed for additional use across the main school network in response to a curriculum request but obviously this eliminates the use of sound, response time being noticeably slow but acceptable.

In both networking situations, response time depends on several factors:

96

- The specification of the workstation.
- The specification of the host file server.
- The topology of the network and loading of cable segments.
- The number of simultaneous users.
- The particular CD-ROM title.

Text-based DOS applications generally work most quickly but lack consistency for integration.

Project Description

Organisation
A programme of raising awareness and acquiring of skills for both staff and students was initiated. Tutors were given a preview session and then all Year 12 students attended a short demonstration, in small groups, with their tutors. (NB: Since acquiring CD-ROM network capability each student has a hands-on session, not a demonstration.) They were given the opportunity to see one disk – ECCTIS – as it was considered relevant to these particular students who were just beginning to think about their Higher Education choices. Also the searching techniques, using the function keys, are straightforward and uncomplicated. ECCTIS seeks to identify the educational opportunities that match the criteria proposed by the students. Data is organised on the disk in a conventional database structure with records organised to facilitate and search. By modifying criteria and exploring new ideas, students gain more information, broaden their knowledge and raise their awareness of the number of educational opportunities open to them. Students also need to develop skills to limit a search which generates too many courses and be aware of techniques which will expand a search that is too narrow.

A supporting guide was produced with clear instructions on how to access the system and ways of using the search facilities effectively.

Small groups of students were also targeted within their subject specialism alongside INSET for the subject teacher. Areas of the curriculum involved were English, Science in Society, Art and Business studies. The emphasis was on encouraging the use of the CD-ROM within a relevant framework and open access was given to all students within the Sixth Form.

Outcomes

Student Feedback
Feedback was gained through student questionnaires, logging use of

available CD-ROMs, discussions with colleagues and students and observations. Typical student comments on the system, such as:

'quick and easy to find information'
'helped me make a quick informed selection'
'much better than using the Higher Ed. filing cupboard'
'why weren't we able to use this last year!'

led me to believe that the objective, to catch the attention of the targeted group, had been achieved. Students were very enthusiastic about the ease and speed with which they could gain information, the ability to progress along lines of personal enquiry and the flexibility to take relevant information away.

Successful use of CD-ROMs involved students in extended decision making. Knowing how to find, select, interpret and reorganise information, critically assess the facts and make use of their findings involves a high degree of conceptual and decision-making skills. Students also needed to be able to develop their evaluative powers to determine what information is relevant and useful.

Transferability of Information Retrieval Skills
Although the majority of students only had initial training using ECCTIS CD-ROM, it appears that they are able to transfer their information retrieval skills to other CD-ROMs even though there is no coherency in the interrogation software. It was found that a high percentage of the students in Year 12 (66%) were confidently using CD-ROM for specific tasks in a variety of curriculum areas. Different searching methods meant that students have to develop different strategies and this can only encourage them to be adaptable and enhance their understanding of the concept of retrieval.

Effects on Styles of Teaching and Learning
The introduction of CD-ROM technology provided the opportunity to initiate changes in the way teachers work with students. A module for Year 12 Art students was produced in which students were given a specific assignment and directed to all relevant sources of information. The changing role of the teacher meant that she became an adviser, and relinquishing control allowed the student to take responsibility of the learning outcome. These new technologies allow a widening of teaching styles and support a move to much more independent approaches to learning. No longer does the teacher have total control of the content or the learning activities. The student becomes more responsible for his/her own learning and takes on a much more active role.

Comment on Gender Issues
Twice as many girls as boys accessed CD-ROM during the logging period. This is somewhat surprising as it is traditionally boys who take on new technologies. The explanations that appear to account for this are that the initial introduction to ECCTIS was perceived as useful and that girls were more keen than boys to investigate their Higher Education options and the possible effect of a 'positive role model' as all the training was undertaken by a female teacher.

Did things go according to plan?
On the whole things were more successful than I had hoped. The value placed by girls on the use of this technology was an unpredicted but beneficial outcome.

Future Developments
With the acquisition of network capability, CD-ROM has been accepted as an everyday resource to be exploited across all subject boundaries. It encourages a wide range of activities ranging from students working independently, small groups to full class exercises. The Sixth form and Years 10 and 11 have access to areas within centrally situated independent learning centres which are wholly devoted to electronic information retrieval.

There have been many specific INSET sessions on targeted CD-ROM, sometimes faculty specific, at other times open sessions where staff come and receive training on CD-ROM they feel are appropriate. Staff are kept informed of available CD-ROMs with a regularly updated guide of CD-ROM titles and a short description of their content.

Liaison links and sharing of resources with our feeder primary and high schools has been encouraged and cross-phase INSET has occurred at the request of interested staff from both our institution and others. Our institution feels there is great value in encouraging and strengthening these links as we can learn from the strategies and approaches adopted in both primary and high schools, where independent and group work are used extensively.

Case Study 3:

Birds of the Ennerdale Valley
Owen Lynch
Ennerdale Primary School, Cumbria
Now at
Orgill Junior School, Egremont, Cumbria

Project Aims and Objectives:
Underpinning this project is the belief that data handling packages can support effective research by primary-school children.
The key objectives of this study were to:

- Develop core research skills including the ability to assess the reliability and validity of information and the source of that information.
- Develop a more refined understanding of basics of data gathering and handling.
- Develop an understanding of the children's role as providers of quality information.

Within this context:

- To develop an understanding of a set of issues relating to birds. The majority of pupils in this sample were very keen ornithologists.

The Class/Students
Twelve children aged between 9 and 11 years (Years 5 and 6) took part in the project. The children were members of a vertically grouped class which included children from Years 3 to 6. This rural school draws from a wide socio-economic background including farming and the professions.

Software	Hardware
GRASS	3 BBC Masters
Newman Software	+ Printer

Project Description

Organisation
The project ran over a period of four terms. During this 15-month period the aims and organisation of the project changed gradually.

Initially a great deal of attention was paid to the framework of the study. The starting point was the children's personal interest in the bird population of their home locality. This was a key factor in the success of the project. The children spent a great deal of time deciding what it was they wanted to know about the birds before the survey was undertaken. They were curious to know:

- Does the size of the bird affected the number of eggs it lays?
- Is there a relationship between wingspan and body weight?
- Do migrant birds lay more eggs than resident species?
- Does the number of eggs laid vary in relation to habitat?

These questions defined the data that the children needed to collect and the structure of the fields for the database. An important point here in the development of the project was the facility to define additional fields after the start of the project. As they came to test their hypotheses, the children became aware of gaps in their information that needed to be filled.

The first act was to list birds which were known to be in the Ennerdale Valley. These birds had to have been seen either by the pupils or a knowledgeable member of the Ennerdale community. The children, working in pairs, then set about finding key facts about their target birds. Information was culled from field observations, talking to local experts and the RSPB, and from standard reference texts.

It was the responsibility of each pair of children to maintain the integrity of the database. Each child acted as the quality-control officer on his or her own data, and for his or her partner's data, at the vital stages of data collection and data input. No information was allowed on to the file until its authenticity had been checked and once entered all entries were re-checked for errors. All secondary sources had to be checked against each other and against primary sources if available. Children had to make judgements about the validity of the data when conflicts between information sources arose, for example if one book predicted a clutch of 4–6 eggs and another 5–7 for the same bird, then a third data source would be sought to resolve the disparity.

Once a significant body of data had been entered the children moved to testing their hypotheses. Information gathering continued throughout the period of the project as the children identified more birds and became aware of the need for additional data to resolve the questions they were asking. This testing phase used minimal computer time. Collectively, over the period of the study, we printed out raw data in tables, scatter graphs and pie-charts which were made into booklets. The children then used these resource booklets to continue their analyses.

Outcomes
The children asked increasingly pertinent questions, not least about the quality of data and the reliability and validity of data sources. They had become researchers!

The children valued the resource they had built both because it stemmed from a personal interest but also because they knew they were contributing to the knowledge base. Contact with experts, and an adherence to strict quality control, meant this was a valid piece of work not just at the school level, but in the real world. This resulted in a developing confidence in their work as the children became aware that they

What is a spreadsheet?

A spreadsheet is a tool to help organise data in such a way that repetitive arithmetic operations can be carried out efficiently. It is a two-dimensional matrix of data, each element of data being located in a space of the matrix. Each of these spaces is referred to as a **cell** and can be identified by its row and column position, rather like co-ordinates on a graph or map. Cells may contain text, numbers or formulae. Cells that contain numerical data are usually organised into categories, with each category of data being entered into one column of cells. It is usual to use the first cell of each column to label the category of data, and hence this cell will contain text. It is not essential but it is advisable to label the columns of data so that the user does not have to rely on the labelling that comes with the spreadsheet package, a rather too simplistic labelling system for children who need to understand what the data refers to. This in-built labelling of rows and columns varies according to the spreadsheet package being used, but most tend to use letters to denote the column and numbers to denote the rows. Figure 7.1 shows part of an empty matrix of a spreadsheet with columns labelled by letters. In the other type of labelling, the letters A to D would be replaced by the numbers 1 to 4.

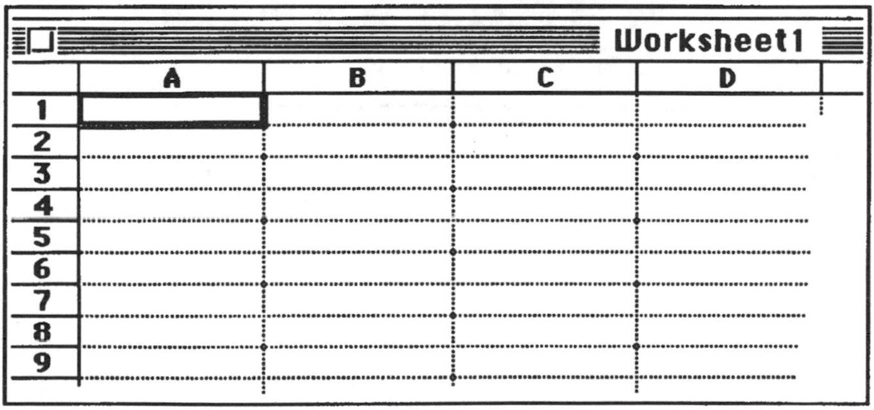

Figure 7.1 An example of a spreadsheet matrix

The number of cells available also varies according to the package used, but the popular EXCEL package, for the Nimbus and Macintosh machines, allows for over 16 thousand rows and 256 columns – more than enough for most classroom activities. Another popular package is GRASSHOPPER for the BBC and Nimbus machines. While some

104

differences between packages exist, such as the convention for entering formulae and the labelling, the underlying procedures and value in using spreadsheet packages remains the same. GRASSHOPPER, which was designed with the primary school in mind, has fewer functions, but this can be a positive aspect for younger or less able pupils as less choice can also mean less confusion. One important difference between packages is with the graphing facilities. These facilities are not always available with the spreadsheet package and data has to be exported to graphic packages. This has important implications for the use that can be made of the tool and I would expect exporting to graphic packages to exceed the expected skills of most primary and lower secondary pupils. EXCEL does contain good graphing facilities (Figure 7.2) and this package is probably the best one available at present for the top of Key Stage 2 and for Key Stage 3 use.

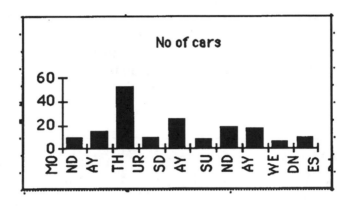

Figure 7.2 An example of one graphing facilities in Excel

The choice of spreadsheet package has to be made by the teacher to suit his or her needs according to the age and achievement level of the pupils, and according to the aims and objectives of the activity for which the spreadsheet is to be used. As mentioned above, some spreadsheets have graphical functions some do not, some have Search and Sort functions; the number of mathematical operations available varies, as does whether the package is mouse driven or key driven, and whether function keys can be used as a quick way to get to menus. These factors affect the complexity of use of the spreadsheet package, and hence will determine the suitability for particular children and their specific needs.

A	B	C	D	E	F
name	test 1	test 2	test 3	test 4	average
MARY	65	54	59	50	sum(b2:e2)/4
JOHN	52	67	62	62	
SUE	39	49	50	47	
DAVID	86	76	79	70	
PAUL	73	57	66	62	
LISA	81	39	53	49	
JO	49	65	59	64	
MIKE	65	78	68	70	
JEAN	55	45	58	56	
LAURA	68	72	72	79	

Figure 7.3 A matrix of data with calculated totals and averages

The most valuable feature of the spreadsheet is that once the data has been entered into the cells, arithmetic operations can be carried out on **whole** rows or columns of numbers. Also several individual cells may be linked together using a formula. For example, in the spreadsheet matrix in Figure 7.3, the cells across each row can be added and divided by four (the number of cells in each row added together) to obtain the average score for each pupil, and this average is calculated automatically by the spreadsheet package once the instructions (formulae) have been entered. The formula does not appear on the spreadsheet once it has been entered. Similarly, if the class average score for each test is required, the cells in each column are added and divided by the number of pupils (Figure 7.4).

	A	B	C	D	E
				Worksheet1:2	
1	pupil	test score 1	test score 2	test score 3	test score 4
2	mary	65	54	59	50
3	john	52	67	62	62
4	sue	39	49	50	47
5	david	86	76	79	70
6	paul	73	57	66	62
7	lisa	81	39	53	49
8	jo	49	65	59	64
9	mike	65	78	68	70
10	sean	55	45	58	56
11	laura	68	72	72	79
12					
13					
14					
15		=sum(b2:b11)			

Figure7.4 A matrix of data showing formula to add column data

It might be useful here to consider one possible application of spread-sheets for younger children based around an activity in which Year 6 pupils are involved with the community, providing tea for Governors and community members visiting the primary school. The pupils have the task of seeing the activity through from beginning to end including costing of ingredients, buying and making the food, and entertaining the guests. The guests visit once a month and the costs of ingredients are likely to fluctuate. As the school restricts the budget available, a spread-sheet (Figure 7.5) is found to be a useful tool to enable the children to decide whether they can afford the same menu each time, and the variability of the total cost of items to buy.

	A	B	C	D	E
1	ingredients	cost per unit	unit type	no of units	cost per item
2	flour	0.49	bag	1	0.49
3	margarine	0.36	250gms	2	0.72
4	eggs	0.72	half doz	3	2.16
5	icing sugar	0.85	kg	1	0.85
6	sugar	0.56	2.2kg	1	0.56
7	bread	0.29	loaf	2	0.58
8	butter	0.98	250gm	1	0.98
9	tuna	0.96	lge tin	2	1.92
10	ham	1.89	packet	1	1.89
11	serviettes	0.65	packet	1	0.65
12	tea	1.12	160 bags	1	1.12
13	milk	1.09	4 pints	1	1.09
14					
15					=sum(e2:e13)

Figure 7.5 The total cost of quantities of items has already been calculated in column E and the formula ready to work out the total cost has been entered

Here, column A contains a text description of the data, in this case ingredients and items for the menu – i.e. flour, margarine, eggs, icing sugar, sugar, bread, butter, tuna, ham, serviettes, tea and milk. The cells across the rows contain the information about the items. So, for example, column B contains the cost of each item, column D contains the required number of units of each item, and column E contains the resulting calculations from the formula to calculate the total cost of each item, then the cell E15 contains the function SUM to calculate the total cost of all items required. It would be easy for the children to change the menu items required, put in the relevant quantity and price and the total cost would then be calculated automatically. The children can provide other formulae to calculate the cost if, for example, cakes only were provided and not the sandwiches, or if only one kind of sandwich was provided (more tuna and no ham, for example). The task could be extended by allowing for varying the number of guests and allowing for reduction or increase in the quantity of ingredients required.

The use of spreadsheets does, therefore, have a clear potential for developing knowledge and skills in the primary mathematics curriculum, while providing the opportunity to start from a real situation – an acknowledged positive starting point for effective learning. Spreadsheets do, however, also have potential benefit to those parts of other curriculum areas that involve investigations such as in science, geography and history. Generally, we can say that if the investigation involves variables (numerical values which change), then the spreadsheet is likely to be a useful tool.

What can spreadsheets do?

A spreadsheet is a tool that can support any activity that involves numerical calculations. In many ways it is better than a calculator in that you can link cells by formulae so that changes in one cell will automatically lead to the alteration of other values in other cells. This is particularly useful where the spreadsheet is used to calculate the total cost of a service or enterprise, such as the cost of a holiday that may have fluctuating fuel or fare costs. Entering the new prices into the relevant cells would lead to automatic re-calculation of the total cost with minimal effort by the user. Studies of weather in which there are several measures that vary over time (temperature, wind direction and speed, rainfall, hours of sunshine, etc.) are another appropriate application for spreadsheets. Children could be involved in taking the measures themselves, entering the data into the spreadsheet and then obtaining graphs to look for relationships and patterns.

It may be that a database could do the job as well as a spreadsheet. Databases and spreadsheets are both useful tools. They both store data in an organised manner, but they differ in their potential use. In the classroom, it is the teachers who will have to decide whether spreadsheets or databases are more useful. If they are more interested in searching and sorting data then a database will probably be the right tool, if they are doing anything which requires them to replicate calculations then a spreadsheet is more useful. In some cases, it can be useful to link both databases and spreadsheets.

There are many possible applications of spreadsheets which renders them particularly useful for cross-curricular activities. The application can vary both in degree of level of use and in the level of sophistication of use. For example, the application may include just simple collection and manipulation of data. Others might include the formulation of a hypothesis and interpretation of results, or may even include modelling, in-depth investigations, looking at number patterns and problem solving. Spreadsheets are especially useful in analysis and discussion of an investigation whatever the curriculum area involved. The readily available graphical representations are useful for investigating relationships. Children can investigate number patterns and sequences through the use of formulae to generate new numbers. By using repeated calculations, pupils can solve number problems.

In school, then, the spreadsheet has the potential to be used in several different ways and tailored to suit different achievement levels of the pupils or students.

Why use spreadsheets?

One clear value of using a computer in data handling is that it processes large amounts of data quickly and easily so that pupils can display graphs and carry out calculations with minimum time and effort. This allows pupils to interact with the data, control how data is displayed, and focus on the interpretation of the data rather than on the mechanics of calculating and graphing. Children who are personally involved in the whole process of data collection and analysis are more likely to understand the data. Primary-school children are quite capable of making complex decisions and of being involved in interpretation of findings given the support of a tool such as the spreadsheet. Without such an emancipatory tool they are consumed by numerous calculations and lose track of the important concepts or issues which are the main aim and objective of the lesson.

Developing skills in the use of spreadsheets

The development of use of spreadsheets in school varies considerably. Some teachers believe it is best to develop the skills gradually, starting with the teacher doing the basic work, and the children being involved in the interpretation of result. Conversely the children might enter the data and the teacher the formulae, before the whole group discusses and interpretes the findings. Other teachers suggest that children should be involved in entering formulae into the spreadsheet from the beginning with the teacher taking on a supportive role. Healy and Sutherland (1991) suggest that pupils should learn to enter formulae right from the beginning of spreadsheet use, and yet they also state that pupils need to be able to use the spreadsheet effectively before pupils can 'exploit the power of a spreadsheet to investigate and consolidate ideas'. Rogers and Barton (unpublished document) recommend that pupils should:

• Learn to manipulate and to graph data in an existing spreadsheet.
• Learn to enter their own data into a spreadsheet with existing headings.
• Then be able to create their own spreadsheet structure to solve a problem.

This leads to the point discussed earlier in the chapter that the way spreadsheets are used in the classroom must be left for the teacher to decide. The previous IT experience of the children will affect their ability to reflect at a higher cognitive level. If children are concerned with pressing the right buttons and finding their way around a grid, then the opportunity for higher level thinking will be impeded. Finding your way around a matrix of cells can be difficult even for adults. One criticism of spreadsheets is that it is easy to get lost – a large number of columns and rows can be used such that only a small portion appears on the screen. Children need to practise moving around a matrix and visualising what the whole looks like before they consider entering algebraic formulae to manipulate the data.

Spreadsheets across the curriculum

Spreadsheets are a tool to use as an aid to investigation. Whatever the curriculum area used as a focus, there are several general steps to undertake during an investigation.

1. Raise a question for investigation.
2. Decide on questions or measures (categories) needed for data collection.
3. Organise data and enter into the spreadsheet.
4. Analyse data.
5. Interpret results (to answer original question) which may lead to formulation of hypotheses.
6. Hence back to 1, raise a question, and through the cycle again.

It is easy to see how the steps above fit into the science curriculum. For example, Rogers describes the use of a spreadsheet for investigating the effect of load on a spring. The data values of mass and length of spring for each experiment can be entered into the spreadsheet. Load and extension can also be set up and plotted using graphical facilities. Pupils are totally involved in the data collection, and are able to obtain graphs to see relationships between variables much faster and more efficiently than if they had to record and produce the graphs by hand.

The use of spreadsheets in scientific investigations is particularly useful for development of skills in the National Curriculum Science Attainment Target 1 – Scientific Investigation. Primary teachers in particular have reported difficulties in providing opportunity for children to develop their skills of scientific investigation, saying that many activities they have tried seem artificial and lacking purpose. In such situations the children have reduced motivation. The spreadsheet provides the means for children to record results, manipulate variables, and to record data and translate into graphical form – all skills from level 4 to 6, and all with the advantage of being able to be derived from a real situation.

Hammond (1993a) describes an activity to help pupils to understand the relationship between speed, distance and time in which the independent variable was the height of a ramp and the dependent measure distance travelled by a toy car. Five repetitions of the test for each ramp height lead to a daunting amount of data for the children to process by hand. Such data can be entered into a spreadsheet, and formulae used to calculate mean distances travelled by the car, also the mean time taken for the car to travel. The relationship between speed, distance and time can then be investigated, and can be compared according to the height of the ramp. Graphical representation of the data would also be a simple extension to help children to investigate the relationship between height of ramp and distance or time of the car's travel. This activity would take a very long time without the aid of a spreadsheet package, and the children could well lose sight of the concept involved.

The most obvious value of spreadsheets is in the curriculum area of mathematics. Many mathematical activities involve long time-consuming calculations which are prone to errors. The skills required to compose and draw a graph from raw data can be complex. While I am not suggesting that children should be protected from, or deprived of, the opportunity to learn and understand how to calculate sums and how to draw graphs, the availability of the spreadsheet can ease these tasks and lead to a more efficient mode of learning and an understanding of higher level concepts than would otherwise be possible.

Time-saving is not the only benefit to the mathematics curriculum. The processes involved in using a spreadsheet can themselves help children to 'see' how number patterns behave, how numbers react under certain operations or use of formulae, and insight can lead to greater understanding and learning. Anita Straker (See Peasey, 1985) suggests that teaching the following mathematical topics would particularly benefit from the use of spreadsheet packages:

- Analysis of statistical surveys.
- Number games.
- Generating number sequences and patterns.
- Calculations of simple and compound interest.
- Multibase arithmetic.
- Probability simulations.
- Investigation of fractions.
- Introduction to the idea of a limit.
- Algorithms for finding roots of equations.
- The bisection algorithm.
- Difference tables.
- Iteration.
- Recurrence relationships.
- Differentiation and integration.
- Vectors and matrices.
- Factorials.
- Taylor's series.
- Newton's method of approximation.

The list is long, and I'm sure other topics could be included. The way in which the spreadsheet is used, however, will undoubtedly affect the learning which takes place. Healy and Sutherland (1991) describes children working at a syntactical level in which children enter code into spreadsheets with little reflection and thought about the meaning of the code. Intervention by the teacher to encourage children to reflect on the processes used is considered to be essential if the experience with spreadsheets is to lead to true understanding and hence to new learning of mathematical ideas. This has obvious implications for how the teacher plans the lesson so that he or she is available to intervene appropriately.

The spreadsheet has particular value when looking at number pattern and sequences. Here, pupils might be asked to generate a number pattern by using formulae. With younger children, they are likely to generate a simple linear function such as altering a column of numbers just by adding a number or by multiplying by one number. For older children, more advanced algebraic knowledge enables them to use higher level functions including quadratics and cubics. This example demonstrates how one activity can be carried out at different levels, according to the capabilities of the child. Using spreadsheets in this way helps the child to build up their understanding of algebraic formulae before they meet algebra in conventional teaching.

As spreadsheets allow a large number of calculations to be carried out at one time, this makes it a useful tool for solving problems using iterative methods such as Simpson's Rule, and Newton Raphson which is part of the 'A' level mathematics course. By using spreadsheets, in preference to a computer, the pupil is able to follow the individual steps undertaken in the iterative process and thus the activity is likely to lead to greater understanding and learning of the mathematical concepts.

The role of the teacher

The examples of the use of spreadsheets across the curriculum, discussed in this chapter, all include investigation work. This suggests that the spreadsheet is particularly valuable in encouraging, and enabling children to work independently of the teacher, and be able to carry out an investigation with minimal support. The pay-off for both pupils and teachers is enormous. Pupils will be able to cover more work in the time available, have opportunity to work at higher cognitive levels, and will be better able to understand the concepts and issues simply by being involved in whole process of data collection, handling and interpretation, but also by supplementing the conventional teaching. The teacher benefits by having more time to devote to children with difficulties, to be involved in the discussion of results, and to supplement their normal teaching practices. Bennett (1991) states that:

> '...computers should be used as a supplement to, not a replacement for, conventional instruction. Secondary mathematics students can be expected to learn more in a shorter time when computers are used....'

The involvement of children in the whole process of investigation work has obvious implications for the provision of hardware and software. If pupils are to remain motivated to carry out a complete investigation, they need to have access to the tools. If the number of machines is a constraint, not only will children become frustrated and unable to complete their task, but the style of management and organisation of the lesson time will also be constrained. Access does not only mean access to a machine, but also access to the software required. Spreadsheets are accessible only if students know how to use them and have experience of using them. Adequate experience in supported lesson time is, therefore, an important prerequisite of independent use.

Summary and conclusion

Many people report that pupils find computer assisted activities to be motivating, making students more attentive and the learning process more stimulating (Said, 1993). Children are better able to learn by being actively involved in solving problems and carrying out investigations than by watching a demonstration by someone else, usually the teacher. A spreadsheet is a tool which can actively involve pupils and thus strengthen the learning which takes place. The application possibilities of spreadsheets is wide and that renders it a useful cross-curricular tool wherever an investigation involving some form of measures and/or calculations is required. It is particularly valuable when used creatively, in that children can 'play' with numbers and investigate how number patterns can be formed by use of simple formulae. The case studies which follow are good examples of using the spreadsheet effectively in the classroom.

Case Study 1:

Statistical Representation in 'A' Level Geography
Will Waters
Gateway Sixth Form College, Leicester

Project Aims and Objectives
The principal aims were to:

- encourage the development of self-study skills and assessment;
- relate the use of IT more directly to the delivery of 'A' level geography;
- introduce students to the use of spreadsheets as a valuable tool for statistical representation.

The Class/Students
Approximately 120 lower sixth (Year 12) students (equal males and females) have taken the spreadsheet module over a 2-year period

Software	**Hardware**
EXCEL 3.0	Two 10-station Nimbus nets

Project Description

Organisation
All first-year 'A'-level students are encouraged to use the drop-in facilities to develop their IT skills. Students are asked to book a 1-hour slot once a week to complete one or more self-study IT modules. The modules are selected with reference to their 'A'-level studies. At the end

of the module students complete a self-evaluation questionnaire.

Once the geography students have completed the self-study module for spreadsheets they are ready to use the tool to support their 'A'-level course. We have devised a number of exercises to support the 'Statistical Analysis' element of the 'A'-level syllabus. The following example is also an investigation of economic modelling.

Indices of Economic Development for 15 Selected Countries

We use many indices (measures) to compare nations' economic development:

* Using the data in the table [*not supplied here*], draw a scatter graph to compare any two indices.
* Describe the correlation (relationship) between the two indices you have plotted on your graph.
* How many clusters of countries can you identify on your graph? Indicate these clusters by drawing a line round each.
* Give a title to each of the clusters identified on your graph. Explain your choice of title.

The data for this exercise is available as an EXCEL file which the students can call up and use.

A second way in which EXCEL is used is to encourage students to evaluate effective and appropriate means of data representation. Using the charting facilities in EXCEL the students are actively encouraged to produce a range of representations of the same data, for example pie-charts and histograms, and to evaluate critically those representations. This use of the spreadsheet's charting facilities has streamlined what for many students was a very time-consuming part of the syllabus. This use of the tool does not remove the responsibility of students to produce valid representations. Line-graphs of non-continuous data such as rainfall are still invalid, however smartly the data is presented!

Outcomes

On the whole students have been positive about this part of the course. They have certainly been able to focus on geographical understanding rather than on the mechanics of data presentation. There were some students who did not apply themselves readily to the new technology and they might be described as computer phobics. On the whole, the students who failed to be motivated by these exercises also failed to be motivated by traditional teaching methods. This is not to say computer phobia is not a problem. These students require careful encouragement.

Did things go according to plan?:
The programme has worked well but there are problems with charting on low-specification machines, particularly with the later versions of EXCEL.

Future Developments
The programme is now a standard feature of our course.

NATIONAL CURRICULUM
IT STRANDS:

INFORMATION HANDLING
MODELLING
MEASUREMENT AND
CONTROL

Chapter 8

Data-logging

Lawrence Rogers
with Bill Morris and Alan Wheelhouse

The term 'data-logging' describes the use of the computer for gathering, storing and displaying measurements from physical sensors directly connected to the computer. This meaning tends not to be recognised outside the field of education, and even within education there are several common alternative descriptors: 'data-capture', 'data-monitoring', and in American parlance 'microcomputer-based labs'. The principal application of data-logging is in the science curriculum where, by tradition, practical activity has flourished. However, its use need not be exclusive to science; it also finds application in physical education (physiological measurements), geography (field work and weather studies), mathematics (motion studies and graph work) and home economics (temperature measurements and physical change). In science the essence of practical work has been the opportunity for pupils to manipulate apparatus, make observations, measurements and analyse results. This chapter will describe and discuss how the computer can be used to amplify and extend these practical skills. It will be argued that data-logging not only provides a versatile measurement tool but also encourages experimentation and exploration of ideas.

Sensors, and interfaces and data-loggers

Apart from the computer itself, these are the basic hardware tools for computer monitoring in practical science. A sensor converts a physical quantity into an electrical signal which is connected to the computer via an interface or data-logger. Most systems allow up to four sensors, of the same or different type, to be used simultaneously. The function of an interface is to make the electrical signals from sensors compatible with the computer. A data-logger performs a similar function, but its circuits are more sophisticated allowing it to collect and store information from sensors, even when it is not connected to the computer (remote operation). For long-term experiments this can be very useful, and also frees the computer to be used for other purposes. Sensors are available for measuring a variety of different physical quantities (e.g. temperature, light, voltage, pressure etc.). Details of their physical properties and mode of operation are found elsewhere (e.g. see manufacturers' specifications).

Here it is helpful to note that there are two fundamentally different types: An **analogue sensor** produces a variable electrical signal which can take many different values between certain limits (usually from O V to 1 V or 2.5 V). Measurement with this type of sensor is very familiar since we are so accustomed to taking a range of readings from conventional instruments such as a voltmeter, thermometer and a ruler. These are all 'analogue' instruments. A **digital sensor** is a switch-type device which produces a signal at one of only two levels, low or high (usually O V and 5 V). These two levels may represent conditions which may be variously described. For example:

ON   or   OFF
TRUE   or   FALSE
PRESENT   or   ABSENT

The commonest examples of digital sensors are light gates, pressure pads, and electrical switches. These are also familiar through their traditional use with conventional electronic stop-clocks and timers.

The two types of sensor lend themselves commonly, but not exclusively to two distinct modes of use: continuous synchronised measurement and single 'snapshot' measurements of events (sometimes used for measuring time intervals) unrelated in time. Most hardware systems allow the simultaneous use of up to four similar or different sensors. The inter-changeability of sensors between different manufacturers' systems is generally quite restricted so the choice of interface or data-logger usually determines the range of sensors which can be used.

Computer measurement

When the computer is used for measurement, the tasks it performs can be summarised as follows:

- Collect data from external sensors.
- Store data in computer memory.

- Display data in graphical form.
- Process data; i.e. perform calculations.

All these tasks can, of course, be performed 'manually' by pupils and at first sight the computer merely automates the process. For many obvious reasons 'manual' measurements have had and will continue to have a dominant role in school science but it must be recognised that there are certain measurement tasks for which the computer offers special benefits which can augment rather than substitute pupils' experience. Many of the benefits arise from the computer's facilities for performing the above tasks at high speed, with large quantities of data over short or very long time periods. Through these, the computer brings certain special qualities to the process of measurement. The following are some of the special features of computer-based collection and storage.

Continuous recording

The rapid repetition of measurements (hundreds of values per second) producing a dense packing of data when plotted on the screen, simulating the continuous recording of results:

- Pupils can observe and measure rates of change.
- Gradients of graphs are conveniently inspected and compared.
- Rapid changes can be precisely monitored.
- Discontinuities and sudden changes are observable, e.g. variation in the voltage across a battery when a load is connected.

Simultaneous recording

Measurements from several sensors collected simultaneously (the sensors may be of similar or different types):

- Simultaneous graphs are conveniently compared.
- Links between different variables may be explored by inspection or by YX plotting.
- Displaying data while being collected reinforces the link between experiment and results.

For example: Temperatures inside and outside a thermal insulation jacket.

Period logging

Collecting data over a period of hours or days: liberates pupil from some of the restrictions normally imposed by the school timetable and working hours. Data may be viewed retrospectively. For example: plant growth, transpiration, fermentation.

Transient logging

• Logging data for short duration time intervals.
• Rapid changes and short-lived events may be recorded in detail.
• Many items of data collected before display.

For example: surge of current when an electric lamp is turned on. Electromagnetically induced currents.

Remote Logging
Collecting data independently from the microcomputer using a data-logger:

• Data-logger may be sited in locations which are not convenient for computers.
• Computer is made free for other activity.
• Well-suited to longer term experiments.
• View data retrospectively.

For example:

• Field work: climatic factors over few hours.
• Laboratory experiments: germination of peas, etc.

Position logging
Collecting data with respect to position (distance or angle). Measurements may be independent of time.

For example:

• Magnetic field around a magnet or coil.
• Intensity of light from a bulb at different distances.

Manual input
Computer logging complemented by data obtained by conventional 'manual' methods. There are certain physical quantities for which the use of the computer is inappropriate and inconvenient. In such cases it is sensible to use the manual method but to provide a means of typing the data into the computer so that it can be analysed alongside logged data.

For example:

• Measurement of mass, length (ruler!), force, etc.
• Oscillation of mass on spring.
• Inverse square law for light.
• Interference of sound.

Delay
Waiting for a specified time before beginning to log data. Starting an experiment after school hours. For example: animal activity during night.

Trigger
Waiting for specified signal condition before logging data. Synchronise logging with a rising or falling signal. For example: pendulum oscillation.

Time and motion

• Measuring time between events.
• Recording the precise times for a whole sequence of events monitored by digital sensors.
• Calculating derived quantities such as velocity and acceleration.

For example: acceleration of a trolley on a slope.

The qualities of measurement listed here show benefits which are largely of a physical or logistical kind. Measurements with the computer are fast, plentiful, prompt and regular, and can be stored and presented immediately. Pupils can observe and measure phenomena in so much more detail compared with the use of manual techniques with conventional instruments; sometimes the computer can make visible effects or patterns which might otherwise be invisible because they are too small, too sudden or too slow. Often pupils gain time which can be deployed on more tasks or more thought. The reliability and 'persistence' of the computer can also reduce the effects of fatigue, carelessness and impatience in pupils.

Display and analysis

The benefits of computer measurement are not confined to methods of collecting and storing data; display and analysis are key features of the 'extra value' which the computer confers on data. These aspects crucially depend on the quality of the software design in providing an appropriate range of facilities which can be easily controlled by the user. In the following discussion, the 'Insight' programs (Leicester University, 1992) will be taken as an exemplary model which successfully exploits the potential of the computer.

The display and analysis facilities fall into three main categories:

- Graphical display.
- Analysing tools.
- Calculating aids.

The display of data on the computer screen, whether this is done simultaneously or retrospectively, can be achieved in a variety of different formats. Chief amongst these is the graph, but results can also be displayed as large digits, as a bar chart, or as a table. Software provides great flexibility in the choice and layout of the display allowing users to adjust the appearance and customise the screen to their requirements.

Features of 'Insight' graphs:

- Choice of size, shape and position of graph.
- Full control over the scaling and labelling of axes.
- Automatic calculation of convenient scale markings.
- Quick interchanging of axes.
- Colour coding of different sets of data.
- Overlaying several sets of data from two or more separate experiments.
- Choice of point size and shape, with a 'join points' option.
- Zoom view, magnifying a chosen portion of the graph.
- Quick switch between magnified and full view of graph.
- Freedom to position the control panel anywhere on the screen.

These features are extremely helpful visual aids which contribute towards interpreting the displayed data. They provide variety and versatility in the manner in which data can be viewed; pupils can experience and devise many alternative views which help them learn more about the data. As with the collecting process, the rapid speed with which the computer performs graphing tasks has a crucial influence in motivating pupils to explore and try out ideas.

In addition to the presentational aspects of data, there is also a need for analysing tools for finding out more from the data, measuring the data, and calculating features of the data. In 'Insight' the analysing aids are all controlled through the cursor lines which are manipulated using the mouse. The cursors make it very easy to select from any part of the graph the particular items of data to be measured.

Measurements using the cursors:

- *Readings –* An instant readout of the data at the cursor position.

Useful for comparing simultaneous items of data and for measuring features such as maxima and minima.

- *Gradient* – For measuring and comparing gradients at different places on a graph and between graphs of different sets of data.
- *Difference* – The vertical displacement between data values on different parts of the graph.
- *Ratio* – Calculates the ratio between two marked items of data to obtain decay constants, half life etc.
- *Area* – Calculates the area underneath a graph between two limits.
- *Time interval* – Shows time relative to a freely chosen origin. Coupled with difference, this can be used to obtain values for calculating average gradients manually.

To help pupils further explore and understand patterns within data and relationships between different sets of data, the computer can be used to generate entirely new sets of data; the new data can be derived from collected data or it can be calculated using mathematical formulae. There are two main purposes for this new data:

- Obtaining derived physical quantities, for example, power from the product of voltage and current.
- Comparing and matching the new data with collected data, for example, curve fitting.

Features of 'Insight' which generate new data

- *Define* – Generates derived data by performing calculations on collected 'primary' data. The calculations are based on simple algebraic formulae which can be chosen by the user.
- *Trial fit* – The user chooses a general formula and the program tries to match the formula to the collected data.
- *Best fit* – Plots the smoothest curve passing through the data points.
- *Average* – Plots a smoothed version of the data; very useful for identifying the trend in 'noisy' or scattered data.
- *Preset* – Plots a function of the user's choice.

When more sophisticated means of manipulating and presenting data are required, data may be exported to other data-handling packages such as spreadsheets, databases and graphing programs. Facilities for transferring and exchanging data between different software applications are very important features of software design.

In general, the collection of single measurements from sensors does not fully justify the use of the computer; most of the advantages described above are associated with the collection and manipulation of large amounts of data. 'Insight' can collect up to 1000 items of data in a regular synchronised manner from each analogue sensor connected. With so much data involved, the graph has the principal role as the method of presenting the data. In contrast, timing measurements using signals from digital sensors are typically obtained from discrete experiments and are unlikely to be assembled in large quantities. In this case the table of results is the principal method of presenting the data. When a graph is required, line-fit facilities are needed to assist in identifying trends in the data.

The implications of data-logging for learning science

Observation, measurement and analysis are at the very heart of practical activity in science. The previous section outlined a variety of features which offer new opportunities for exercising these skills and, in turn, these have implications for the way in which pupils can learn from practical work. They also provide teachers with new opportunities for managing pupils' activity. The computer facilitates a shift in emphasis away from the mechanical collection of data towards its interpretation; this leaves time for more attention to be given to observation.

Studies of pupils' performance provide evidence that pupils start with qualitative responses in investigations (APU, 1988) and appear to be disinclined to adopt a more quantitative approach which would increase the complexity of the experiment. There is a need to develop pupils' ideas about the value of quantitative evidence for greater reliability, communicability and repeatability. Here the computer has great potential by providing an experience which can progress from qualitative to quantitative. For example, the immediate display of a graph, while results are being collected, provides pupils with a qualitative overview of the data without the need of handling numbers or tabulating data. Pupils are freed from the labour of processing numerical data to obtain the graph image. This makes the graph a starting point rather than an endpoint in evaluating the results. Quantitative analysis of the data might be a subsequent activity, but initially pupils can inspect and select what is of interest on a graph, and appraise its significance. For example, the effect of the scales on the shape of the graph may be explored and pupils might be persuaded that to understand these changes the calibration of the scales needs to be investigated. They can be introduced to the quantitative properties of the data when the need arises. For pupils with very limited skill in plotting graphs accurately, this represents a considerable increase in the quality of the information available to them.

Experiments on the topic of 'motion' provide numerous examples of the special benefits of prompt measurement and calculation. Derived quantities such as velocity, acceleration and kinetic energy are available instantly, inviting exciting innovations in teaching approach. For example, pupils may explore directly how the kinetic energy of a toy car rolling down a slope is affected by factors such as distance travelled, angle of slope, mass of car and friction; this is without the need of numerous calculations. The minimal delay between doing the experiment and seeing and evaluating the results encourages an interactive approach; pupils might first speculate about the results and then test their prediction.

Patterns in data are readily revealed when displayed visually. Maximum values, minimum values, a general trend, smooth changes, sudden changes, rates of change all show up clearly on a graph. Studying the curvature or straightness of a graph gives valuable information about the connection between the quantities plotted. 'Insight' provides a useful method of exploring trends in data and relationships between physical quantities through curve-fitting facilities (Average, Trial fit and Preset). With these, pupils can devise or choose a simple mathematical model for a relationship and test it by matching the curve or straight line to the actual data. Although the computer performs the necessary calculations and plots the curves, pupils have an important creative role as they exercise judgement in selecting a model or formula, and adjusting parameters and constants.

To make effective use of sensors and computers, it is not necessary to adopt a revolutionary style of teaching. When taking the first steps in using a computer in the laboratory, many teachers feel most confident in using it simply as a demonstration aid. It has a number of benefits to offer this traditional role. A successful demonstration requires good communication and interaction with pupils. The computer can assist this by allowing the whole class to observe experimental effects on a bold and colourful screen display. Again, the computer's 'real-time' display process can greatly speed up discussion of the results. Analysing aids and curve-fitting facilities simplify the process of searching for patterns and meaning in results. Within the science curriculum there are many examples where practical difficulties limit what can be achieved by teachers and pupils. For example:

- Attempts to find evidence for Newton's Laws of Motion often falter with ticker-timers which generally demand a great deal of skill to achieve convincing quantitative results.
- Measuring changes of state and cooling curves by reading a thermometer with a compact scale every 30 seconds for 20 minutes demands great concentration and may even preclude qualitative observation.
- Investigations on the characteristics of electrical components generally require excessive repetition of measurements.
- Measurements of plant growth are limited by the confines of the laboratory and school timetables!

Although there is no panacea, sensors and computers can help to overcome some of these difficulties:

- Light gates connected to computers give pupils access to high-quality measurements of velocity and acceleration.
- Temperature probes can simultaneously monitor four cooling liquids and free pupils to watch physical changes.
- A multitude of electrical measurements can be collected and displayed in a short period.
- Growth, light, temperature, etc. can be monitored round the clock inside or outside the laboratory.

Many modern science courses encourage pupils to explore their own ideas through 'investigations' in which they are given a large measure of responsibility for the design and conduct of experiments. Some advocates of this approach emphasise the value of encouraging the interaction between the pupil's knowledge, practical ability, commitment and creativity (Woolnough, 1991). A complementary view is that investigations foster a spirit of inquiry which encourages pupils to make better sense of the world and act on this understanding more effectively (Claxton, 1991).

With the establishment of the National Curriculum for Science (DES, 1991) there is a clear endorsement of an investigative approach and the curriculum guidelines identify the skills required for 'exploring science'. These are the ability to:

1 Plan, hypothesise and predict;
2 Design and carry out investigations;
3 Interpret results and findings;
4 Draw inferences;
5 Communicate exploratory tasks and experiments.

The Orders give detailed guidance on the type of activities which characterise an investigative approach, and several roles for the computer are indicated. The Programmes of Study for each key stage are explicit about the use of computers for measurement and suggest several types of activity for which software is ideally suited. For example:

At Key Stage 2 activities should:

- Involve the capture, transmission, storage and retrieval of information using computers and sensors.
- Promote the search for patterns in data.
- Foster the interpretation of data, and evaluation against the demands of a problem.

At Key Stage 4 pupils should be encouraged to develop their investigative skills and understanding of science in activities which:

- Give opportunities to use information technology to gather and display data from experiments.
- May take place over a period of time and may require sampling techniques.
- Encourage the systematic recording and presentation of data using, as appropriate, a full range of forms, including graphs and mathematical relationships.
- Encourage pattern searching in complex data and predictions requiring abstract reasoning.

One of the most valuable roles for the computer is the means that it provides for reducing the skill level required for the mechanical aspects of measurement activity. A successful investigative approach involving problem-solving relies on low-level skills which do not require much thought but rather are effortless and as automatic as possible. The lack of automism interrupts the problem-solving process and can lead to errors (Underwood and Underwood, 1990). Computer software simplifies the measurement process by managing issues such as the frequency of measurements, labelling and scaling the graph axes and plotting and storing the data. It can be argued that this empowers pupils by reducing the level of skill required and lowers the ability threshold required for successful use. This can result in building confidence and competence in investigative work for a broader range of ability of pupils.

Unfortunately, this is easily defeated if the software and hardware tools themselves possess a strongly 'technical' appearance and feel. Hardware requires the minimum of wires, sockets and technical labelling. It is very necessary for software to be designed for a range of users with different levels of skill and confidence in computers. For the novice, results must be easily obtained with the minimum of fuss; for the sophisticated user, the software must meet the demands of complex tasks and special requirements.

Data-logging in practice

So much for the theory about the advantages of data-logging to practical science in schools. In practice, a disappointingly small number of science departments have implemented its use in any substantial way. A survey by the National Council for Educational Technology (NCET, 1993) has reported that only 11% of secondary schools used data-logging for more than 3 hours per year, 54% made some use and 35% made no use at all. At one time, limited resources and the lack of easily used sensing equipment were blamed for the poor uptake of the technology, but in recent years the situation has changed (DFE, 1992) and the more significant obstacle has been the insatiable demand for in-service training by teachers (NCET, 1993). Teachers' confidence has still to be won and perhaps the supposed advantages are insufficiently understood to convince teachers that the investment of effort is worthwhile.

A recent study has closely observed the use of data-logging in several classrooms in three comprehensive schools and has compared the outcomes with conventional practical work (Rogers and Wild, 1993). Pupils were given tests which attempted to discern learning from the lessons involved. Observation schedules were used by independent observers to monitor the type of pupil activity on a time interval basis. The results of most of the written tests were inconclusive, showing hardly any differences in performance between pupils using computers and those without computers. However, the evidence gathered through classroom observations did show that the use of the computer had a significant effect on:

- The quality of pupils' results and their presentation, particularly in the context of graphical interpretation.
- The time spent on collecting results and making observations.
- The quality of the ensuing small group discussion.
- The stimulus and opportunities for follow-on activity.
- The balance of activities appropriate to the conduct of investigations (planning, recording, hypothesising and reporting).

The most positive effects indicated by the study mainly relate to the character of pupils' activity rather than measures of their achievement. It was reported that pupils using computers had, compared with their non-IT counterparts, been observed to spend more time discussing their results. It needs to be noted, however, that the use of computers alone could not assure this; the teacher had a crucial role in developing pupils' skill to discuss effectively. The software merely provided the tool for prompting discussion and inquiry. Teachers are well aware that the social interactions within groups play an important role in determining the success of the work. Investigative work thrives on a more fertile supply of ideas and a wider range of skills than does directed activity and thus benefits greatly from group work. It has been shown that co-operative groups perform more accurately than competitive groups or individuals. Group work demands discussion which is of great value in allowing pupils to learn from each other and explore ideas, but certain social skills, a willingness to help each other and a tolerance of peer guidance, are required for successful collaboration (Claxton, 1991). The teacher has a special responsibility to cultivate an atmosphere where these skills may develop and flourish.

Pupils also need a strategy for exploring their ideas. For the teacher, the management of open-ended tasks is a sophisticated process which cannot be left to chance. Trial and error is a weak strategy for solving problems: it does not incorporate a way of producing good guesses about what might work; and the 'error' runs the risk of making matters worse before pupils hit on a fruitful line of inquiry (Claxton, 1991). Pupils need a framework (Rogers, 1992) which helps them employ their knowledge and skills to:

• Define research questions.
• Identify and think about variables (the concept of 'fair test' is a productive strategy.).
• Design experiments.
• Plan the action.
• Make and test predictions.
• Evaluate and interpret the results.

Thus, the effective exploitation of the opportunities afforded with IT depends upon the teacher adopting positive strategies. When successful, the emphasis may be shifted away from the performance of the more mundane tasks of laboratory work towards encouraging pupils to test and extend their understanding of the science involved. Lesson time needs to be devoted to developing the new skills employing IT and gaining a good working knowledge of the software to use it to its full potential. However, with well-designed software, the amount of time actually needed to achieve an efficiency threshold can be quite modest. In Case Study 1 it was observed that many pupils became uninhibited in the use of the software and hardware after about only two lessons.

In the Leicester/Loughborough study (Rogers and Wild, 1993), teachers' views were sought on the essential conditions for 'successful' IT based lessons, and the following consensus emerged:

*   confidence of teacher;
*   quality software (easy to understand and use);
*   reliable sensors (When the signals are noisy or intermittent, pupils can be misled.);
*   standard connections (achieved by using a single type of hardware);
*   clear system for organisation of equipment in the laboratory (storage and distribution of data-logging kit; computer stations);
*   time for teacher and technician to supervise and maintain the IT kit;
*   training of the technician to gain understanding of IT requirements – a whole-school policy so that pupils have complementary IT experiences across the curriculum.

The above evidence suggests that the success of this educational innovation is not likely to depend on the merits of the technology and pedagogy alone, but also on a complex combination of factors which include teaching approach, suitable training, level of resources, methods of implementation, supporting agencies and institutional policies.

Case Study 1:

Use of Data-Logging in the Study of Weather
Alan Wheelhouse
The City Technology College , Kingshurst, Birmingham

Project Aims and Objectives
The principal aims were, first, to cover relevant parts of the Science National Curriculum, and, secondly, to assess the impact of data-logging methods on the achievement of the pupils in gaining understanding of the topic and developing process skills. At the end of the unit of work pupils would be tested against statements of attainment relevant to the study of the weather such as temperature, rainfall, wind speed, land and sea breezes, air pressure etc. The class would be observed to identify patterns of activity which are dependent on the use of the computer.

The Class/Students
The Year 8 class consisted of 24 pupils of mixed ability spanning a broad range from 'high fliers' to one boy who was statemented for special needs . The cultural background was predominantly white with a small minority of Asian and Afro-Caribbean children. The social background was very mixed, the area of the college being

very much 'working class', but there was a significant number of 'middle class' pupils within the group.

Software	Hardware
INSIGHT, Longman Logotron	3 Acorn Archimedes 420 computers running under Risc OS version 2 with 2Mbyte RAM a 40mb internal hard disc. Standard 14″ colour monitors
INSIGHT is £69 for a single user copy and £330 for a site licence.	Each group had a LogIT data logging unit with a range of sensors (temperature, humidity & position). shared an Epson dot matrix printer

Project Description

Organisation

The class was split into two halves, trying to avoid any gender or ability bias. One half used IT exclusively for the collection and analysis of data whilst the other half performed exactly the same experimental work using manual methods of data collection and analysis. Very similar worksheets were designed for each method so that there was a consistency in the instructions.

The tasks set over the series of lessons varied from a fairly rigidly controlled experiment where the variables were prescribed, to a number of 'open-ended, team-based, problem-solving' experiments where the groups used the skills that they had acquired during the project to complete the work or solve the problem. Pupils' performance was assessed by two methods:

* Observation by both staff from the college and by university researchers.
* Written tests on graphical analysis set before commencement and after the completion of the unit.

Outcomes

Pupil's learning

The test results showed that both groups of pupils improved their knowledge of the topic during the three or four weeks that they studied this unit. The pre-test showed most pupils' knowledge as being at around level 4 in National curriculum terms. By the end of the unit every pupil had improved this by at least a level and the best improvers by three levels, coping confidently with work at level 7. Classroom observations indicated high motivation amongst pupils, perhaps reflecting the British fascination with the topic of weather. Many pupils kept weather diaries during the project and one girl even video recorded Australian weather forecasts over the Christmas holidays for comparison with Michael Fish and Suzanne Charlton.

The software
Pupils had not used INSIGHT before this unit but had been trained in the use of other RISC OS software which gave them confidence in exploring the menu structure and using the WIMP environment. They could consequently explore many of its features intuitively without having to be shown how to do so. The use of INSIGHT was undoubtedly motivating; its presentation was clear and the standard of its graphics excellent. Pupils took to INSIGHT far more readily than the non-RISC OS software supplied with the hardware. Once they had discovered its zoom and analysis features the pupils then took delight in being able to make much more detailed comparisons between sets of data.

The style of learning
The teacher's philosophy embraced the view that 'the pupils are co-owners of lessons' and therefore in planning a series of lessons, an attempt was made to vary the type of lesson, ranging from a prescriptive style at the start of the unit to very open-ended, problem-solving, team-based style at the end. Pupils were extensively 'consulted' about their previous experience and what this meant in terms of what they would do next.

Did things go according to plan?
As far as possible, the teacher and technician tried to pre-check all the equipment before lessons began, and fortunately only minor problems occurred. The software gave no problems, and the hardware problems were confined to connecting leads being pulled out at inopportune moments and batteries going flat occasionally. The hypothesis that the use of IT helped pupils gain a better quality of experience in lessons was supported by independent observers. Their observations showed that pupils using computer graphs spent a lot longer on discussing their results, analysing trends and scrutinising errors. In contrast, the manual method of collecting of data was much more time consuming; pupils were neither experienced enough nor organised enough to combine data

collection with graph drawing, and they therefore completed their graphs after collecting data. This immediately put them behind the IT groups who not only had time to analyse their graphs but also to repeat the experiment if necessary to try and replicate something that they had observed. Also, because of the large quantity of data collected by the LogITs, pupils achieved smooth curves; this was far from the case with the 'manual' groups who generally took readings at 1 minute intervals and often missed interesting features.

The main organisational problems were:

- The increased demand on the teacher's time to ensure that the equipment was set up and functional.
- The spatial organisation needed to get IT equipment, LogITs, probes, bunsens, glassware etc. on to a worktop so that they could safely be used. The move towards notebook sized laptop computers may help this space factor.

Future Developments
The effect of working with the pupils as a team had a profound effect on learning in the group. The quality of outcomes was boosted by the use of quality tools, so the experience was well worth repeating. However, in a future project the IT and non-IT groups may be better organised as two parallel classes rather than splitting one group in half. It would not be necessary to change either the hardware or the software. To use an upgraded Archimedes running under RiscOS3 or with Arm3 would convey a speed advantage, but is not essential. To have a printer at each station, say a bubble jet which is quiet and produces a high definition output, would be a big advantage. The LogIT probes were excellent, and when used in conjunction with INSIGHT produce low 'noise' and therefore produce data that is much easier to analyse.

The project began to show an improvement in the understanding of graphs. The pupil tests showed that most pupils were able to take numerical data from the graph or describe trends. Many, however, were moving towards extrapolation, interpolation and then going further by making predictions based upon altering a variable. It is in this area that further work could be done, developing more sensitive indicators in the hierarchical skills of graphing.

The further manipulation of data could also be explored. INSIGHT is a versatile tool because it allows graphs and data to be exported in standard file formats that can then be inserted into DTP packages and spreadsheets. This means that clear, high-quality graphics are available for manipulation and display. Also with the facility to import as CSV or

SID files, there is the possibility of comparing theoretical with experimental data. This for a biologist would be superb, as living material is subjected to the effects of far more variables than purely physical phenomena. The software holds the promise of providing a truly interactive experimental modelling tool.

Case Study 2:

Motion Studies within the scheme of work on Forces
Bill Morris
Whitley Abbey Comprehensive School, Coventry

Project Aims and Objectives

- To introduce the concepts of speed, velocity and acceleration and the factors which affect these variables.
- To use computer-assisted data-logging to gather data.
- To compare computer-assisted methods of measuring velocity and acceleration with conventional methods involving ticker timers.
- To investigate pupil–pupil and pupil–teacher interactions during practical work.
- To analyse pupil's written work.
- To examine pupil's verbal responses to the use of IT compared with the conventional methods of measurement.
- To evaluate the impact of data-logging on the teaching and learning of science.

The Class/Students
Pupils from two Year 9 mixed-ability science groups studying a topic on Forces which includes introductory work on motion. Pupils are taught as Tutor Groups in Year 9 so the ability range is wide. The range of cultural/social backgrounds were similarly mixed, with approximately equal numbers of boys and girls. The National Curriculum levels across all four attainment targets ranged from 3 to 7.

Software	**Hardware**
SENSE and CONTROL software, Educational Electronics	Acorn Archimedes A3000 one set of data-logging equipment standard digital light gates

Project Description

Organisation
Because of the limited availability of data-logging equipment at the

time (only 1 complete set of S&C), the IT-based work was organised as part of a 'circus' of experiments. This meant that small groups of pupils (usually four in a group and usually single sex by the pupils' own choice), rotated through a range of activities on or related to motion. Thus one group used the ticker tape whilst another used the IT, and then they swapped round the following lesson. The lessons lasted 70 minutes which usually gave pupils enough time to write their work up before the end of the lesson. The IT-based work took place in a small IT laboratory adjacent to the main science lab, because the A3000's were not situated on trolleys. The pupils thus took the science to the IT rather than the other way round.

Outcomes

Most children acquired a reasonable working knowledge of the basics of motion and some of the factors that affect velocity and acceleration such as mass of trolley, angle of incline and force applied. It was not possible to establish the relative contribution of the IT to the learning process but the views of pupils were sought through questionnaire and interview techniques. Pupil performances in the end of topic test were not significantly better than those in other Year 9 groups.

In the questionnaire, pupils commented that the main advantages of using IT in motion studies were that there was a significant time saving and they were able to carry out a much greater number of measurements. With the ticker tape, most pupils managed only one or two 'runs' down the slope and spent the rest of the lesson analysing and cutting up the tape. However, some pupils commented that the ticker tape was a good way of learning about changes in velocity and acceleration because this could be seen as a visible change in the distance between the dots on tape. Many pupils commented that the computer method was more accurate, and they were more willing to trust the computer than the ticker tape. Pupils also liked the fact that the computer could store their data and work out derived quantities such as average velocity, and '0–60' conversion, automatically.

There was a certain amount of novelty in using computers. The equipment was perceived as 'high-tech' which was a significant motivating factor. Many pupils commented that they would be more inclined to experiment with the use of IT to gather data in future science lessons, and that their overall confidence in the use of IT had improved as a result of the motion work. A significant number suggested that computers made science lessons more interesting and enjoyable, and most wanted greater access to IT in the future.

Pupils generally liked the organisation of the 'circus' of experiments because it allowed them to work at their own pace with minimal teacher involvement. Very little prompting was required in the extension work in which pupils were asked to investigate, open-endedly, the factors that affect acceleration.

The 'Sense and Control' software was colourful and easy to use although the colour graphics are of no obvious advantage in digital work of this nature. The step-by-step calculation of velocity and acceleration was generally well appreciated.

Single-sex groups of 3 or 4 were the preferred groupings. Most pupils questioned thought that the quality of their work had improved as a result of using IT.

Did things go according to plan?
There were no obvious problems related to conceptual understanding. I remain convinced, however, that the conventional methods of measuring velocity and acceleration should not be dispensed with in favour of IT-based methods. The IT augments and enhances the traditional methods and offers the facility to carry out multiple experiments with a fine degree of accuracy. There is something to be said, however, about the value of counting dots on ticker tape.

Organising this kind of activity around one set of kit is less than ideal, but this did not present any problems in terms of organisation or management. There were, however, only limited opportunities for groups of pupils to work collaboratively.

The only real technical problem encountered was the influence of 'stray' light on the performance of the light gates with 'Sense and Control'. On one particularly sunny day, the equipment had to be moved to an adjacent room which had the luxury of blackout.

Future Developments
IT in the science curriculum at Whitley Abbey has now taken off, partly as a result of the successful NCET Portable Computers in Schools bid. It is now possible to take the IT to the science with total flexibility in terms of management of hardware. We now also have the luxury of multiple sets of data-logging equipment and a wider range of more powerful software including INSIGHT which offers much greater versatility in graphical display and derived functions over 'Sense and Control' software.

INSIGHT is now being adopted as the standard data-logging software, and opportunities to extend IT-based activity into schemes of work are being constantly reviewed.

Future work will focus, amongst other things, on a more statistically valid evaluation of the impact of IT on teaching and learning in science including a more comprehensive analysis of pupil interactions and longer term cognitive development.

Chapter 9
Control technology

Peter Whalley
with Jeff Buckles[1]

'*Computers and Lego are only for boys!*'
(Jessie, aged 11)

This was my (loud) introduction to the use of control technology in the classroom, my daughter had just had her first experience of *control-*Logo. From this inauspicious start, Jessie's teacher[1] and I attempted to develop a form of teaching control technology that could provide a more satisfying and comprehensible experience for all the children. The first part of the chapter reviews the general purposes, practices and problems of teaching control technology, whilst the second outlines an alternative approach based on the ideas of object-orientated programming that are starting to become accepted in education. Finally, more general ideas about teaching control are discussed in terms of a wider conception of computer literacy.

What is control technology?

Control technology involves the use of a microcomputer to control physical micro-worlds such as traffic lights, lifts, level crossings etc. (Figure 9.1). It can provide an interesting and powerful educational experience, and has been viewed as a good way to provide practical experience of programmable systems that are familiar to children. The essential components of a control technology system are:

- The *control language* running on
- a *microcomputer* linked to
- an *interface* unit which controls
- a *microworld* of motors, lights and sensors.

---

[1]Jeff Buckles gives his version of events later in the case studies.

138

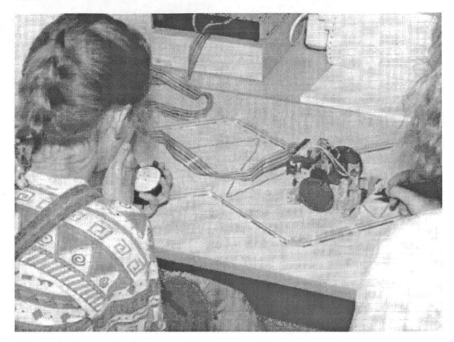

Figure 9.1 A typical control 'microworld'

The first experience that children generally have of control technology in the school is the use of a 'floor turtle' such as the *Roamer* which combines all four elements in one package. Turtles or 'buggies' as they are sometimes called are probably the most widely used control microworld in the classroom (see Figure 9.1). This is due at least in part to historical reasons which, as we shall see, continue to cause problems for the teaching of control today. Turtles moving about on the floor were originally conceived of as an extension of the 'screen-turtle' that is the drawing tool of the LOGO language, and their prime purpose was related to the teaching of mathematics or LOGO itself rather than having anything to do with control as it is presently conceived.

Subsequently children are likely to work with one of the control versions of the LOGO or BASIC programming languages on a micro-computer, e.g. CoCo, control-LOGO, Contact 2000, etc. Figure 9.2 shows the programming interface to the SmartMove system which, like some of the others, incorporates a graphic resemblance of the external control box. The initial projects tackled by children usually only involve the computer controlling 'output' elements such as lights and motors; with the sequence initiated from the keyboard. The idea of 'sensor' elements triggering off some chain of commands, e.g. to open a sliding door, is then introduced. More complex forms of 'feedback', e.g 'line

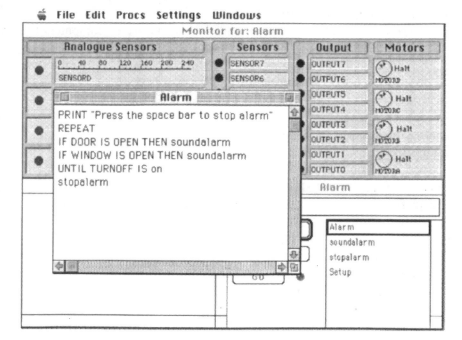

Figure 9.2 The SmartMove interface

following' or temperature control, are usually not introduced until secondary school because of the programming complexity involved.

Teaching control

The teaching of control technology can be divided into four main topics:

- *Building* the mechanism to be controlled.
- *Linking* motors and sensors to the interface unit.
- *Developing* the control program.
- *Considering* the wider implications of control.

Whilst it is possible to take a class sequentially through these topics, there are strong arguments for treating them separately. Some children will be much more adept at building the mechanisms than others and a few will be intrigued by the logical 'bit testing' involved in making the computer–microworld links. However, it seems unwise to make interest and success at these early stages a precondition for tackling the last two topics, as these have the greatest educational significance for most children. It appears that girls can be particularly disadvantaged by the badly structured teaching of control technology.

A review of research into attitudes towards and use of computers by Hoyles (1988) showed how markedly girls were tending to avoid courses involving computer use and that the trend seemed to be becoming progressively worse. The gender issue has dogged the use of control technology since the early 1980's, when computers first began to appear in the classroom. This is due at least in part to the fact that control technology tasks were very often used in the experimental studies that showed girls to be 'failing'. The author must admit to scepticism about some of the research in this area. Lack of persistence in some of the rather trivial tasks set might just as easily be given a positive interpretation as a negative one. However it seems clear that an apparent 'failure' with control tasks could affect girls, who might have been performing just as well as boys on other IT related topics such as the use of word processor or drawing packages. The author's own research in this area (Whalley, 1992) shows that the apparent gender difference in 'programming' ability disappears once the topic is taught at an appropriate level of description, and in a way that takes account of the girls tending to be less familiar with the mechanisms being controlled in the microworld – in effect de-emphasising the lower level aspects of control.

A recent HMI report has confirmed what many practitioners have suspected for some time, that there are significant difficulties with teaching control in the classroom and that proportionately very little time is being spent on it (Welsh Office, 1992, p.12). The author and others (e.g. Owen, 1993; Whalley, 1992) have argued for some time that one of the major causes of these problems in actually making control technology work in the classroom is the unfortunate choice of serial programming languages, primarily derivatives of LOGO or BASIC, on which most control technology systems have been based. Some of these issues and their possible solution will be developed in this chapter.

Programming and control

The original 'push' to get micros into UK schools seemed at times to be premised on the idea that if the nation's children could be taught to program in BBC BASIC it would somehow revitalise our economy. As we have generally moved from being computer *programmers* to computer *users*, these ideas seem more and more misplaced. Owen (1993, p.112) has pointed out that whilst the whole nature of programming has changed, inertia in the educational system has caused it to not be able to keep up with developments; and particularly so in the area of control technology. The form of control technology with which we are probably most familiar in the home is the video recorder, where a stored program of times and channel selection is made to control a tape mechanism. If having to 'program the video' has ever caused the reader difficulty then you already have some insight into the difficulties posed by the control technology systems presently used in the classroom.

Early in the 1980's, The British Computer Society advised that the use of 'flowcharting' as an aid to programming be dropped as it was not a good representation of the structured programming methods being used **then**. Yet it is still common to find flowcharting being used to teach control technology, and commercial control languages based on flowcharting displays are still being introduced. We can be quite certain that the programming languages in use when children at school today enter employment will be several orders of magnitude 'higher level' than those we have now. It is therefore important that any work in the classroom that is related to programming be focused on the conceptual issues involved, and to not become sidetracked by problems of irrelevant detail. This is a problem that seems to be particular to control. Perhaps because those involved in developing other areas of the IT curriculum have been less intrinsically interested in the technical problems, they seem to have managed to free themselves more successfully from such constraints.

Figure 9.3 indicates the way that a program to control a level crossing would be developed using a series of procedures and gives some idea of the syntax of control-LOGO. The syntax or 'level of description' used with control technology problems does not match the childrens' needs. The idea of a buggy 'turning left' or a lift 'going up' are intuitively comprehensible. It **is** possible to teach children that 'bit 1 ON' and 'bit 5 OFF/bit 6 ON' can mean the same things, but it is a quite unnecessary complication. The historical reasons for the 'bits and bytes' approach to control technology, particularly in the UK, lie in the origins of the topic as an offshoot of the 'microelectronics' program. Obviously if you are teaching about electronics then it might be necessary to drop down to 'logic levels' and 'bits', although even this has been questioned (e.g. Owen, 1993, p.109).

The problems caused by the use of syntax that is unnecessarily off-putting are quite independent of the language chosen. It is easy in any of the commonly used languages such as control-BASIC or control-LOGO to set up meaningful procedure names, it is just that this is not common practice. This must be partly out of conservatism, but it is tempting to think that some would worry that without the syntax of 'bits & bytes' control technology would not look 'difficult' enough to be

```
TO TCOMING
IF INPUTON? 1 <STOP>
TCOMING
END

TO LFLASH
REPEAT 10[SWITCHON 1 PAUSE 0.5
SWITCHOFF 1 SWITCHON 2 PAUSE 0.5
SWITCHOFF 2]
SWITCHON [1 2]
END

TO BDOWN
SWITCHON [3 4]
PAUSE 5
SWITCHOFF [3 4]
END

TO TGONE
IF INPUTON? 2 [STOP]
TGONE
END
```

Figure 9.3 Breaking a problem down in control-LOGO (part of a program)

taken seriously. This need not be the case though. With the syntactically simple 'buggy' language described later in this chapter it is quite easy to set problems that will tax an adult's understanding of control issues.

Object-orientated control

As we have seen, the most obvious problem with the common control languages appears to be their syntax, the language of input and output 'bits'. However a more fundamental problem for control languages is that they must be able to deal with the **simultaneous** actions of multiple objects. If they cannot do this then they risk conceptually distorting the control problems, and making them unnecessarily difficult for children to solve. Papert, the creator of the LOGO language, outlined its deficiencies with regard to parallelism more than 10 years ago. He claimed that there are:

'... two reasons why a computer system for children should allow parallel computation or "multi-processing". First from an instrumental point of view, multi-processing makes programming complex systems easier and conceptually clearer. Serial programming breaks up procedural entities that ought to have their own integrity. Second, as a model of learning serial programming it does something worse: it betrays the principle of modularity and precludes truly structured programming.'

(Papert, 1980, p.222)

Clearly Papert's first reason is important. The choice of procedural control languages does result in an unnecessary complexity when attempting to deal with simultaneous events, and attempts to patch some form of parallelism onto existing control-LOGO or control-BASIC languages results in a syntactic complexity that is even more difficult for children to understand. However, the second reason he gives is the more fundamental; the procedural languages impose the wrong metaphor for creating control environments. Moving to an object-orientated formalism makes it possible to switch from the metaphor of the executive endlessly looping through a list of checks and actions, to that of independent actors operating in a modular fashion; responding to events, and communicating by messages when their tasks are complete. This metaphor is much more easily comprehensible to children as it more closely maps the actual problems of control environments. A simple example that conveys the flavour of how the object-orientated

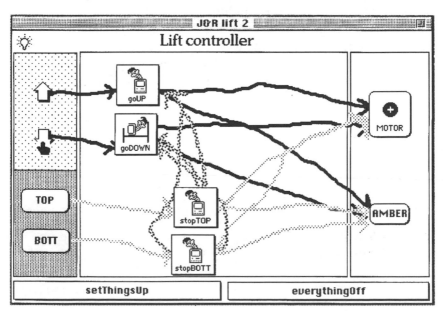

Figure 9.4 An object-orientated control interface

144

approach to programming differs from the procedural is to think of a
single person going round a supermarket with their shopping list as
against a family shopping; each member with their own list, but
bringing their 'finds' back to the one trolley.

A more computer related example of the object-orientated approach
are the 'modeless' interfaces of the Macintosh and Windows systems[2].
As far as the user is concerned, they can click on any 'button' or pull
down any 'menu' item instantaneously. The underlying serial nature of
the computing device that they are using has become effectively transparent to them. The same object-orientated metaphor can be applied to
control languages, making control problems much easier to understand.
The control interface of a 'space lift' shown in Figure 9.4 exemplifies
this approach. The basic structure of this form of control environment is
simple to construct in one of the new graphic 'scripting' languages such
as HYPERCARD or VISUALBASIC. Each object in the control
microworld can be assigned to a 'button', and each button can then be
given the 'script' to be carried out by that object. As the children add
sensors or motors to the microworld, they drag into their control space
an appropriate input or output actor. The advantages of this form of
control language is not that they are computationaly more effective, but
that they are **conceptually** more effective. A simple lift control system
designed with a procedural language is likely to be just as good – the
difference will only become apparent as the model becomes more
complex or when it has to be modified. When, for example, it is necessary to disable inappropriate controls, or to be able to stop at intermediate floors once the lift is moving.

The case studies written by Jeff Buckles compare his classroom
experience with control-LOGO and the object-orientated HYPER-
BUGGY[3] control system. The HYPERBUGGY system was developed
to match the natural progression of ideas in the National Curriculum
Document relating to the way that control technology should be taught:

• Control by *direct instruction*, e.g. of a *Roamer* or another child in
  role-play.
• The idea of having to give *precise commands* to the computer.
• Control by a *series of commands* from the computer, e.g. to a buggy.

The HYPERBUGGY interface allows the user to move to and fro
between these levels as required by the problem. The 'scripting', or

---
[2] It is important to realise that the ideas underlying 'actor' based languages date back to the 1970's.
They have existed for as long as LOGO and BASIC, it is just the advent of 'windowing' software
environments that has made them more accessible.
[3] A commercial version of this system is to be made available by TAG Software in early 1994.

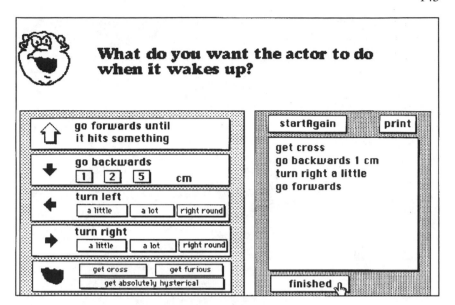

Figure 9.5 The programming interface of the HYPERBUGGY system

programming, level (shown in Figure 9.5) is made available to the children on the screen, and also on card in a format which exactly matches the layout and syntax used on the screen. The children are thus able to work out all the scripts and 'talk through' them before entering anything into the computer. This system and details of experiments with it are described in more detail in Whalley (1992), but the essence of the way it works is that sensors ('feelers' to the children) on the front of the buggy send messages to the actors, which in turn send messages to control the separate wheel motors.

Classroom control

Researchers and advisers working with one or two children at a time can appear to make almost any system of control technology work. The author once tried to make this point at a conference by making the light-hearted remark that given enough effort, and one teacher per child, it would be possible to teach them to program in FORTRAN. It turned out that the next speaker had done just that. The real test is whether it is possible to make control work in the classroom whilst being responsible for a whole class, and this is where systems involving a complex syntax like control-LOGO fall down. Control technology can really only be considered to be working in the classroom if the children can operate as inde-

Figure 9.6 Planning scripts using a cardboard 'editor'

pendently as they do in other curriculum topics. The expedient of having 'supply' assistance for the class teacher is obviously possible, but would require a very high valuation of the worth of teaching control in relation to other topics.

The curriculum document (DES, 1990, p.45) provides as one example of a control task a child giving 'commands' to another, who would presumably be acting as if a robot. Such use of role play as an introduction to the ideas underlying control technology will appeal to many children and teachers – and it also saves on the equipment budget! Figure 9.6 shows children using a 'cardboard' editor to plan scripts for the actors in the HYPERBUGGY system. In this way several groups may work quite independently, and with little teacher assistance, planning and testing ideas before entering them into the computer. Instead of spending much of their time simply encoding the children's ideas, the teacher's role in the control lesson changes to become much as it is with other topics, a problem poser and discussant.

The physical constraints imposed on most computer based work, such as a single keyboard and mouse, can make for difficulties in paired work. Whilst working with a partner has many positive aspects, other 'problem solving' topics would not tie the children together to the extent of their having to constantly share the same pen and piece of paper. The author's early experience with control in the classroom was that pairs of girls tended to co-operate (and end up with both of them having their hand on the 'mouse'!), whilst boys were prone to 'turn taking' (paying little attention when not in control). It is necessary to ensure that the control activities really do require the attention of both children if paired work is to succeed. This was taken into account in the design of the HYPERBUGGY system and its classroom materials to the extent that not working co-operatively makes the task considerably more difficult.

An exception to the notion of paired work always being a 'good thing', and one which applies to problem solving tasks in general, is where the solution requires a single 'flash' of insight. An example from the HYPERBUGGY task is where the angles of the maze are made more acute and the children have to make a counter intuitive modification to the program that they have just spent an hour or so developing. The time taken for children working alone to solve this part of the task can vary between a few seconds with no hints, to twenty minutes with several hints provided. Joiner (1993) has shown how the interaction and dialogue between children whilst solving many computer based problems can be very constructive – even when it sounds just like arguing to the outsider! However it seems that this may not be true for all problems. One pair of girls, who had struggled with the task for 10 minutes when working together, each solved it in seconds when working apart. The advice to teachers was consequently modified so that each pair was split up whilst they worked on this part of the task, but were subsequently asked to 'merge' their separate solutions into one control program. Many of the suppliers now provide quite voluminous packs of information for use with their control technology systems. None the less it is important that the practising teacher should always keep in mind the question of how the materials would work when they are are engaged with the whole class rather than just quietly working through the exercises by themselves.

Control in the 1990s

It is a pity that many children do not have a more positive experience of control technology in the classroom because the issues relating to the general uses of control in society are very important. Working out ways of testing control systems so that they can be guaranteed to be 'foolproof' and to function perfectly for many years is a significant challenge for engineers, and is of course an important issue for the rest of society who have to suffer the consequences of any failure. As this

148

148

chapter was being written there were newspaper reports of how one group of 'experts' had declared that the control programs of a particular nuclear reactor were now so complex that they were impossible to fully check. Only days later the American Airline Pilots Association were expressing concern that attempts to correct minor faults in 'autopilot' software (which requires three control computers to be constantly checking each other) might lead to even more serious problems.

This wider aspect of the teaching of control is emphasised in the curriculum document attainment targets for IT, *'They should be able to make informed judgements about the application and importance of information technology, and its effect on the quality of life'* (DES, 1990, p.43). It is therefore even more unfortunate that the HMI report referred to previously noted that *'... scarcely any time is set aside for the evaluation of computer applications or the ramifications of IT usage'* (Welsh Office, 1992, p.12). Of all the IT topics control is perhaps the best suited to informing the discussion of these issues, helping children to develop personal views about the role and use of computers in modern life. Aspects of 'testing to destruction' are an important part of the control lesson, and can be be designed into the classroom materials so that these general implications can be appreciated. The challenge of 'Can you make it go wrong?' can be guaranteed to bring on incredible feats of diligence, even extending into break-time. Within minutes someone will have left a car under the descending arm of the level crossing, and then driven a train into it! The children building the 'space lift' controller described earlier had to quickly modify it so that the switches became 'locked out' in certain positions, or else risk having to rebuild the lift every time someone kept their finger down constantly.

It is an interesting phenomena that children who are quite unsure whether a buggy will get through the maze when they are carrying out a program 'by hand' can suddenly become convinced that it will get through when the same program is being run by the computer! Perhaps in the same way that control technology was originally perceived as a vehicle for teaching programming, it might now be thought of as a way to gain insights into more general aspects of computer literacy. In particular it can provide concrete, and personal, opportunities for the demystification of the computer. For example, within a 'safe' environment children can experience the *programmer's fallacy*, of constantly assuming that the next modification is bound to work. And even more important, an awareness that whilst the computer might posses superior abilities in terms of patience and exactness, it was they who had the imagination to 'see patterns' and actually find solutions to their problems.

Case Study 1:

Using LegoTechnic
Jeff Buckles
Deputy Headteacher
Heronsgate County Combined School, Milton Keynes

Project Aims and Objectives
The principal aims were to:

• develop an understanding of control technology;
• stimulate problem-solving behaviour.

The Class/Students
32 Year 7 pupils from a socially mixed Combined School (5–12)

Software	Hardware
Lego Control	BBC Master
From most educational	
suppliers	Lego Interface A
e.g. Commotion	Lego Technic Buggy

Project Description

Organisation
A class of 32 Year 7 pupils from a socially mixed Combined School (5–12) in Milton Keynes were given control tasks using a buggy constructed from Lego Technic. The buggy was controlled through a Lego Interface A connected to a BBC Master using the LEGO CONTROL LEGO language. (This is available from most educational suppliers, e.g. Commotion.)

Outcomes
Before the pupils could begin to move the buggy there had to be a lot of teacher input, explaining the language of LEGO LOGO. This meant that the teacher had to be present with the group for long periods in order to explain the language and to ensure that it was typed into the computer correctly. When pupils began to enter their own commands, if there was an error it would require the presence of the teacher to go through the program looking for errors. This was very demanding on pupil time and did nothing to foster independence in the pupils. The lack of visual stimuli on the screen and the high incidence of programming errors lead to some frustration. The LEGO LOGO meant that the emphasis was on the programming and not on getting the buggy to move. It also meant working at one level, the issue of progression being one of complexity rather than moving in stages.

Did things go according to plan?
The project was not as successful as we had hoped.

Future Developments
After the initial experiment the Lego buggy has been used
with a hand 'battery-box' controller as an introduction to
control for younger children.

Case Study 2

Using Hyperbuggy
Jeff Buckles
Deputy Headteacher
Heronsgate County Combined School, Milton Keynes

Project Aims and Objectives
The principal aims were to:

• develop an understanding of control technology
• stimulate problem solving behaviour

The Class/Students
32 Year 7 pupils from a socially mixed Combined School (5–12)

Software	Hardware
HyperBuggy control	Apple Mac Classic
from TAG Software	Resource controller
	Fisher Technic Computing
	Experimental Kit Buggy

Project Description

Organisation
The same pupils as in Case Study 1 were given control tasks using a
buggy constructed from the Fisher Technic Computing Experimental
kit. The buggy was controlled through a Resource Controller attached to
an Apple Mac Classic. The HYPERBUGGY control software is based
on the HYPERCARD programming language. (A version of this software with a pre-constructed buggy and interface is available from TAG
Software.)

Outcomes
The HYPERBUGGY program presented the pupils with a visual interface on the screen to control and program the buggy. Because the
program worked on three levels it was possible to put it into direct drive
and ask the pupils who could get from one end of the maze to the other

the quickest. All that was needed was some preliminary instruction on the buggy. The teacher was then able to move on to other pupils. The second level of early programming still allowed the pupils to work almost independently, using a series of programming cards. This allowed them to seek out patterns in their programming so as to be able to move the buggy down the maze. The third level of programming allowed the pupils to build upon the previous work and to enter their own programs and then see if they worked. The experience from levels one and two meant that if a programs didn't work at this level it could be corrected quickly. The emphasis was on controlling the buggy initially, then moving onto programming with a more 'natural'language.

Did things go according to plan?:
We felt that this project was successful and that we fulfilled our aims.

Future Developments
Since the first trials the HYPERBUGGY system has been taken up by other teachers at Heronsgate. It has now been used with three classes of Year 7 pupils with great success.

Chapter 10

Multimedia and learning: Normal children, normal lives and real change

Stephen Heppell

Multimedia – a bad term for a good idea

In the mid-1990s there are few more contentious words than either Multimedia or Learning. Learning has a long history of impassioned debate and currently 'learning productivity', 'flexible learning', 'distance and autonomous learning' and 'learning' with many other qualifiers is at the heart of much current educational controversy. Multimedia has a much shorter history but as we attempt to separate the hype from the hope, the reality from the rhetoric, it is no less controversial. Multimedia, of course, describes the possibility that a computer might at last be able to deliver all the elements that we take for granted in the rest of our everyday lives: speech, text, graphics, video, music, sounds, data.

Around the world is it not surprising that we find education itself at the heart of much impassioned debate, when, as is currently the case in almost every education system in the world, we speak of making change happen in schools, colleges and universities. A chapter title that encompasses multimedia, learning and change might expect to offer, or at least confront, contention. However, as we have focused our gaze on obvious technological and pedagogical change the real revolution has been in our children and their everyday lives. This chapter is centrally concerned with that change and with the need for education to recognise, and offer strategies to progress, the emergent capabilities of our young 'children of the information age'.

Multimedia of course is a strange word; media is already a plural and adding 'multi' to it didn't help much. 'Integrated media' might have been better but the word has a very brief life and has already burned brightly in its supernova stage before being consigned to the same bin as many of the other 'techie' words that once seemed so important in our computer lives. Multimedia only seemed important as a word when few computers offered the capability that the word seemed to describe. When every computer offers multimedia capability (as will rapidly become the norm) the word will die for ever. No one seriously describes life as a multimedia experience, although it is, but we do have special words to describe our lives where key information elements are missing – sensory deprivation, blindness, deafness, dyslexia. In the same way, a text-based, command-driven computer might well be described as visually impaired and mute. In our everyday lives, missing any of the multiple media components that comprise our normal information channels will be characterised as exceptional. In our computing lives (in 1994 at least) the multimedia computer, with most of those multiple media components in place, is seen as the exception, worthy of special terminology.

Because of the concept that multimedia is somehow exceptional, when we come to consider the computer and learning, the debate focuses on the occasions when adding video, sound and other elements might be useful. What extra contribution might video make? How might auditory icons offers the signification of cues and clues that characterise good interface design? Logically it would be more sensible to assume that, as is the case in our everyday lives, all these elements would always be present. We might then ask in what circumstances might it be appropriate to leave something out (when should we exclude text, or when might video be abandoned for example), to good effect. If life is generally a multimedia experience, our normal, computer based, learning environment should be too.

As an illustration, in the 'Playground Physics' section of the pioneering Visual Almanac[1] computer driven interactive videodisk, learners watch a sequence showing a merry-go-round changing speed as children move in and out from the centre. Initially the video sequence of a merry-go-round moving is played with a soundtrack where pitch, but not tempo, offers clear clues for the initial observer. Later in the same 'module' the music is abandoned in exchange for a real time graphical representation of the merry-go-round plotting speed against time. Careful design decisions had been made to exclude some of the rich variety of multimedia channels available to focus children in their learning. The discipline for the designer was what to leave out rather than what to include. Curiously, although we have had multimedia around our learning environments for something like a decade it seems

---

[1] Visual Almanac was developed at the Apple Multimedia Lab, San Francisco.

154

often that, with a few honourable exceptions, the debate about multi-media design and application has been characterised by discussions about what is technically possible rather than by what is pedagogically desirable and in what context.

Learning and its analysis, of course, has a far longer history of debate. We can be reasonably clear from a vast weight of research that elements like need, intention, creative participation and delight may be key components in successful learning for many children whilst self-esteem, clear goals, autonomy and supportive critical friendship may be key motivators. However, looking at much multimedia courseware as a learning resource it is too often impossible to derive any intended learning outcomes and still more difficult to see how users may participate creatively, with delight, by these new learning environments. Worse still, the needs and intentions addressed by the software are often, sadly, those of the designers rather than the intended users. In short: over a millennium or so we have developed a variety of fairly clear ideas about some of the components of successful learning but there is little evidence that many these have been absorbed by other than a few commercial multimedia designers.

'How children learn?' is complex enough, but computers have added a new urgency to debates about: 'what do they learn?', 'how do we know that they've learned it?' and 'what do we assess?' At present some national education systems are struggling with the dimensions of these problems, while rather more countries are struggling to be aware that they are issues; none yet have solutions.

A simple analogy is illustrative. Imagine a nation of horse riders with a clearly defined set of riding capabilities. In one short decade the motor car is invented and within that same decade many children become highly competent drivers extending the boundaries of their travel as well as developing entirely new leisure pursuits (like stock-car racing or hot rodding). At the end of the decade government ministers want to assess the true impact of automobiles on the nation's capability. They do it by putting everyone back on the horses and checking their dressage, jumping and trotting as before. Of course, we can all see that it is ridiculous, yet in schools all round Europe we are arming children with spreadsheets and assessing the same old mathematics capabilities, we are arming them with collaborative, mutable writing tools, like word processors or desk top publishers, and then assessing them individually as writers through a typically linear writing form that is increasingly frustrating for them. In the UK we have even gone as far as to ban some of the powerful tools from the assessment process – having supported writing, appropriately, with spelling checkers and thesauruses we then remove them at the point of assessment. In terms of our analogy we take away the car and put them back on the horse, in time for the test. Patently foolish. Allowing children to author multimedia essays and assessing their performance with a hand-written summative test is equally foolish.

Whilst much of our focus on multimedia has been essentially a technical one, we have at least noticed the rate of change of technological platform that is supporting our young learners. ULTRALAB houses the National Archive of Educational Computing and browsing the archive it is impossible not to marvel at the progress from teletype to 24 bit screen, from punch tape to optical media or from solitary 'beep' to 44 kHz stereo sound. There has been real technological progress in two short decades and power per price has dramatically improved at the same time. This progress has become a topic of interest in its own right; throughout Europe TV programmes offer weekly presentations of technological progress and we regard ourselves as technologically literate if we can simply keep up with the key milestones of progress. But, as we marvel at the rate of change of the hardware and software we bump up against surprises that we fail to understand or interpret: children seem unable to focus continually on a TV screen for an educational broadcast, seem less willing to be absorbed by literature, find no place in their lives for narrative radio. Typically we interpret this with a deficiency model of the child – they have become information grazers, their concentration threshold has collapsed, they have accelerating levels of illiteracy, parents send them to school unexposed to textual culture, and so on.

Similarly, whilst we are absorbed in the debate about what children learn and how we measure it, we focus too often on deficiency – nations publish endless reports contrasting (unfavourably) the arithmetic skills of young learners with previous eras, or with other cultures, but in doing so we again fail to notice, or log, changes that are occurring in ordinary children. Might it be possible that children are developing new emergent capabilities as information handlers? Might we be seeing not a decline in their capability but a change in the skill set that represents that capability? If so, we might hypothesise that it is not in hardware and software but in normal lives and in normal children that we will find the real revolution that is changing our learning and multimedia futures.

What might some of those changes in normal lives and in normal children be? In the 1950s, in Europe, television was unusual. It was the Radio Age. The generations that currently dominate our teaching professions were the children of this radio age. They retained the habit of reading too, as an important information and entertainment source. Cinema was not an everyday experience and was most significant socially, as a night out. This 'radio generation' were fed linear narrative information in a largely passive form. Families would gather round the radio and listen to favourite programmes together. TV, when it finally became available for mass consumption, needed darkened rooms, offered a tiny grey and white picture and was again a primary narrative source. As TV developed, many houses evolved their social rooms to give the television a central focus. TVs were often built into a massive piece of furniture with all chairs facing towards it. Advertisements and programmes were dominantly narrative in form.

However, TV in the 1990s provides an information window in a much greater information context. Children watching TV in 1993 might have a Nintendo 'Game Boy' in hand, a photo-magazine on their lap and even, inexplicably to parents, be watching whilst listening to their 'Walkman' headphones. Of course, all this will be with the channel controller nearby and often with a vast number of channels on offer which are 'stepped through' at frequent intervals. Children seem to 'graze' information and TV production companies, hoping to retain the interest of the youth viewer, seek to build programmes with little narrative structure, but with complex information dimensions – text, voice-over, video-edited with great rapidity, separate background projection, music and graphics. Watch advertisements aimed at children for any number of convincing examples. Interestingly, market research and evaluation seem to suggest that for the adolescent viewer problems occur not with the complexity of this programming style but only when the content delivered across these complex information dimensions is too bland and unchallenging!

In schools this manifests itself as a crisis in educational broadcasting as children find it increasingly difficult to sit for 50 minutes and offer their undivided attention to a single information source with no other choices and no video controller. This is not a collapse in concentration thresholds as the deficiency model of the learner would have us believe, it is the result of children's hunger for information autonomy, for their right to focus information attention where they choose. Of course, teachers and parents have changed too; it is equally uncomfortable for their teachers now to sit around a radio, doing nothing else, and listen to a single aural source, although for any born before 1950 this was once a normal part of family entertainment. We have all changed our media habits and our capabilities as media consumers. A group of children were asked for suggestions about ways of making prison less attractive and more deterring (a common focus of interest in the politics of 1990s

Britain!). Amongst many ideas was one from a young girl who suggested that to: 'give them black and white TV and no way of changing channels', would be as close to hell as she could imagine; there is no shortage of similar powerful anecdotal evidence of the extent to which the climate of expectation that we bring to our media lives has changed in some 25 years.

There is considerable irony in this for multimedia. We have struggled technically to be able to deliver the full screen narrative form that TV so clearly represents – one hour of full-screen, full-motion video has been a multimedia 'holy grail' for so long! – and yet just as we appear to be able to deliver it, we find that what learners seek is something else anyway. They need a browsing, grazing environment where learner autonomy is fundamental, where the model of information represented is crucial to that browsing function, where metaphor and interface design are of primary importance and where sound bites, video snatches, auditory icons and text labels offer a complex and participatory environment that challenges the learner and recognises their increasing sophistication as information handlers and creators. Our normal information lives have changed without us noticing and the implications for multimedia and learning are complex and significant. The many publishers seeking to provide electronic books and narrative CDs are seeking to generate product that is a generation too late, as the age profile of buyers clearly indicates.

And what of other changes in ordinary children's entertainment lives? Computer games are of real cultural importance to this 'information generation' and games have now developed the same short fashion lives that pop music once had. From parents and the print media today computer games get the same sort of critical press that 1960s pop stars and the 'rock generation' once got: children can't read because they play too many computer games or watch too much TV. The games allegedly immerse them in violence and gender stereotypes as virtual heroines queue up for actual rescue; children become hopelessly addicted, social misfits, trapped in an electronic never-never land. Children have fits, are exposed to pornography and truant from school. Or so we are led to believe by the same deficiency model of children that is applied to their learning lives.

Ironically, many of these wild and improbable claims are made by the same generation that was, in its own youth, supposedly corrupted and debauched by Mick Jagger's antics in the 1960s. They ought to know better and, just as our focus on technology neglected crucial changes occurring with information consumption, so our focus on what is wrong with the games has led us to neglect important and valuable

158

emergent capabilities, and new expectations, in the children playing them.

Games can provide a challenging problem solving environment where players observe, question, hypothesise and test. Games can offer a vehicle for collaborative endeavour and, crucially, they have changed the climate of expectation that surrounds children's computing experiences. Children expect delight, mental challenge and a role that is evolving from interactive to participative. Everyone acknowledges anecdotally that children are competent and astute computer users. Few designers of 'educational software' for young learners begin from this premise. If multimedia learning environments are to offer challenge, provide delight and deliver real learning outcomes they must first recognise the emergent capability of learners and respond to the climate of expectation that those learners bring to their computer screens.

What might we conclude from all this?

Firstly, as we look to engender real change by harnessing multimedia technology in our learning environments we might be more aware of the cultural change that has already occurred and might seek to move forward not from a deficiency model of the changing learner but from a position that seeks to recognise and value emergent capabilities.

Secondly, acknowledging, identifying and progressing emergent capabilities of learners might lead us to look through fresh eyes for new learning outcomes. Again, real change is likely to occur not by trying exclusively to deliver old learning outcomes with new technology but by looking for new learning outcomes that can only be delivered by that new technology.

Finally, there is much that we already know about good learning and it is incumbent on good software designers to reflect more of that understanding than has so far been the case. It does appear that our young learners can actually serve as critical friends in the design process and part of our acknowledgement of their capability might include involving them, the users, better in the design process as well as the user testing (see case study below).

Case Study 1

In 1993, at ULTRALAB, we were interested in the fusion of ideas that might result from asking children, teachers, parents and our own software team to design a piece of software. What would the children look for? What good experience might teachers bring? What did parents want? What could learning theory contribute to make it all work better?

As a test we took a very simple learning outcome – remembering the multiplication tables. This was a 'know that' rather than 'know about' learning outcome; it was very discrete as a target but it was easily tested too and children, teachers and parents are motivated by any solution which delivers a faster learning of the tables. Multiplication tables offer the key combination of need with intention.

What happened, and how did 'X' develop?

Firstly, the children's input. They already had (as is typical) good experience of computer games and other 'home computing' activities. This had developed a 'climate of expectation' amongst them. They knew what motivated them, what delighted them and what held their attention. They were very aware as software critics and full of good ideas.

Children wanted:

- A high score record – they were particularly astute about the need for the score to allow their peers to compete when multiplication capability varied between individuals.
- Colour, sound and great graphics.
- An interface that it was obvious how to use – they suggested that opening screens of 'what to do' text would be unnecessary if the screen was designed well.
- Pressure to keep them on task but also because 'racing' against a pressure environment was exciting for them.
- Good rewards – something that said 'well done' and had a bit of variety in it. They wanted 'well done' but they didn't want it to get in the way of their 'playing' and slow everything down.

The children did not want:

- Delays – anything that got in the way of performance was unwelcome.
- Loads of 'how to use it' text. They could see from their own prior experience how a game worked and wanted 'X' to be equally obvious to use. This was very important to them.

Parents were less ambitious in their requests, but they did want:

- The software to work and actually help children to learn their multiplication tables. Parents were very goal focused in this respect.
- Some way of allowing children of different ages to compete against

each other even if one was on the 4 times and another on the 9 times multiplication tables.

Teachers had long experience of teaching tables. They wanted:

- The software to achieve its learning outcomes (!) and actually help children to learn their tables.
- Some clear indicator of which numbers were being multiplied on the 'table grid' for reinforcement.
- The random 'asking' of the tables so that children could not step through by adding for each subsequent answer.
- An opportunity to explore the grid first before being tested on it.
- Some easy way to stop and give up if things were going badly.

Teachers did not want:

- Better sounds for 'wrong' than for 'well done' (too many programs that they had seen rewarded failure with the best sounds and animations!!).

Of course, ULTRALAB is concerned with learning and learning theory suggested that:

- Children needed visual and aural cues and clues to help reinforce the memory task.
- If the clues and cues are created by the children, 'ownership' will help them learn.
- Intention and need are both important. Children have a need to learn their tables. They need this learning to deflect the pressure that they suffer from not knowing them. Almost universally they are tested at school on their multiplication tables retention. If we could combine this need with personal intention then the simple learning target might be achieved very quickly. Personal motivation can be developed from the delight that a 'games' environment can offer.

Taking into account this good advice from children, parents and teachers, we developed 'X' as a Hypercard stack using QuickTime for its music and animation (Figure 10.1).

The software does most of what was asked of it by the teachers, parents and children; it offers visual cues which can be painted by individuals as they work their way through the software, but it doesn't yet offer aural cues and clues because we wanted to find out how well the visual ones worked first. It doesn't offer printouts because we decided that the learning outcome was table capability and that was what children took home or into school. We did not want to focus on the pictures as an end in themselves, they were only a means to an end.

Figure 10.1

Initial testing suggest that 'X' seems to work rather well. The combination of children, teachers and parents as designers showed that they all had something to offer 'learning'. As a case study it throws interesting light on the process of software design and the role of children in the developmental process.

An interesting by-product of this small project was to discover that the traditional rote way of learning multiplication tables masks how few sums actually need to be remembered – after the easy 1 to 5 and 10 times tables have been removed and allowing for commutativity (2x4 and 4x2, etc.) there are really only 10 'hard' sums to remember and four of those are square numbers that children seem to find easier to recall.

Parents (and teachers) found it useful to help children realise from the outset that commutativity exists and that the whole task of remembering multiplication tables is manageable with only 55 sums in total to be completed. Because of the way that children traditionally learn their tables, for many there is simply no understanding that 3x7 is the same as 7x3. Ask a child who has learned their three times tables what three sevens are and they will usually say 'I don't know'. 'X' makes commutativity explicit and for many children simply realising this seems to halve the task they have in front of them. It's a great morale booster!

'X' has been made available on ULTRALAB's 'Insights for Teachers and Parents' CD-ROM for Apple Macintosh computers.

Chapter 11

Some Reflections: Is all right in the IT world?

Jean Underwood

At first sight, the figures from the DFE's most recent survey of IT provision in Secondary Schools (March 1992) make cheerful reading. The survey shows that the number of computers in schools continues to rise. In 1990 the average number of microcomputers in secondary schools was 40 but this had risen to 58 in 1992: an increase of 45%! Over the same period, the student to computer ratio had improved from 18:1 to 13:1. Total expenditure in 1991–92 on IT equipment rose to almost £60 million, or £21 per student. Promising though these figures are they hide a genuine resource problem. Only 14% of the machines in the survey had hard discs, and Acorn BBC Bs and the most basic of the RM Nimbus range accounted for nearly 40% of all machines. The positive figures of the survey are founded on a time-bomb of ageing equipment.

What are implications of relying on ageing hardware? Even now that hardware is beginning to fail. As that failure takes place, the current level of new money will only maintain rather than improve ratios. Writing off equipment from the school audit and damaging student:computer ratios may not be acceptable to hard-pressed school managers in this brave new world of LMS (Local Management of Schools) with its emphasis on competition, rather than collaboration, between neighbouring institutions. In my own institution we are cannibalising defunct machines to keep a dwindling pool going. Many, but not all, schools will be in a similar position. It may take some time before a realistic ratio of machines to users is known!

Reliance on ageing hardware means that many schools are using, and in the case of one local authority's primary schools *currently* buying, hardware which no longer has any relevance to the workplace. Even more significant than the mismatch between school and workplace is the mismatch between hardware and new software developments. Those schools dependent on old BBCs and Nimbus 186s find themselves cut off from new developments. In Chapter 5, Simon FitzPatrick introduced 'KidPix', a simple painting package, aimed at younger age groups. This program, which is now available for both Apple Macs and PCs, uses the full sound and graphics facilities of these machines, and is very memory hungry. It simply is not possible to give young children such easy to operate programs on old hardware. In my own chapter (Chapter 6) I talked of new databases, such as BODYMAPPER, which demand a much higher specification of machine than often found in schools. It is not simply that these new programs are more 'glitzy', although that is certainly true. They are frequently much easier to use than the old software. A case in point would be the separation of the graphing and search/sort facilities in OURFACTS and the smooth integration of such facilities in say CLARIS WORKS or PINPOINT. This ease of use makes them more available to both the student and the teacher and allows the user to focus on the content area rather than on the nitty gritty of driving the program. This is clearly shown in Peter Whalley's chapter (Chapter 10) on control technology.

Old hardware is not necessarily bad or useless. It has its place. I know of at least two university research projects that are being run very successfully using the datalogging potential of BBC Masters. Electronic mail can be sent using the most basic of kit (Chapter 4) and one of our local mathematics department is happily running MULTIPLAN on its RM 186s to develop students' understanding of number patterns. It is the geography or economics departments that require good charting and graphing facilities to make spreadsheets come alive for their students (Chapter 7). Science departments can use simple hand held data loggers to capture information but should they want their students to formalise the data or to produce models then a computer with good, memory hungry software is a must (Chapter 8).

Other areas in which the older hardware is no longer viable include many of the tasks for the Communication Strand of the National Curriculum (Chapters 3 and 5) in which layout and design, rather than simple text processing are becoming critical skills. And courseware covering even basic topics such as multiplication are now presented in new and novel ways to children (Chapter 10) to both arouse the learners' interest and maintain their concentration, but also to provide them with an active tool to think with.

I am arguing that many children or students have a restricted choice of experiences because of the quality of the hardware available to them. Sweetman, however, goes much further and claims that some GCSE students are likely to achieve poorer grades because of the quality of hardware in their schools.

'In a typical school, sharing sixty ageing computers between six hundred pupils, it is clear that the two hundred or so pupils who are working towards key stage 3 assessment and GCSE may be in danger of getting a level or grade which reflects the quality of the equipment they use and the access they have to it, rather than their ability in this area.'

(Sweetman, 1993, p. 96)

This is a very gloomy prognosis indeed. Although, as Sweetman points out, as the current tests of IT are paper based a theoretical understanding of IT, rather than an any ability to actually use the kit, may be all that is needed. Questions such as that for Level 8 (Information Technology Strand) – why is it easier to misuse computerised information than that stored on paper? 'is so open ended ... that almost any half relevant answer can be justified.' (p. 97).

Resource levels are not the only issue facing us, however. Sir Ron Dearing's review of the National Curriculum has left all of us uncertain as to future role of IT. His current pronouncements suggest that will we go back to IT skills and possibly even computer studies, under a new name, rather than maintaining the goal of permeation of the whole curriculum. Does this matter? In those schools were IT is well established and the use of the technology is already engrained then the spur of National Curriculum may not be needed for future developments to take place. Here the teachers and students know that IT is a valuable resource for learning. But in those schools were the IT co-ordinator is fighting an uphill battle for credibility, and equally importantly for resources, then the lack of a national imperative for IT will result in a withering of the use of the technology.

The chapters in this book represent a progress report on the tool use of computers in our schools. Here are a number of examples of effective classroom practice across a range of subjects and in a variety of schools. The linking concept for all of these chapters is the enhancement of our students' learning. The beneficial effects of that tool use lie in an understanding that there is a right tool for a job; that tools must be used for purposeful activities and not simply to gain practice with the tool; and that tools are essentially there to make life easier for us. They should enhance our skills or speed up our performance. A tool is both emancipatory and an amplifier of our performance. If the use of a tool does not achieve these objectives then there is little point in using it. We hope these experiences will encourage the wary to recognise the value of IT in the classroom.

References

APU (1988) *Science at Age 15.* London: HMSO.

Aspin, T. (1990) *Spreadsheets in the Mathematics Classroom.* Hatfield: Hertfordshire County Council.

Austin, R. (1990) Electronic mail in a European setting. In Marshall, D. (ed.) *Campus World 1990/91.* Cambridge: Hobsons PLC.

Azmitia, M. and Montgomery, R. (1993) Friendship, transactive dialogues, and the development of scientific reasoning. *Social Development,* 2, 202–221.

Balacheff, N. and Laborde, C. (1984) Langage et symbol et preuves dans l'Enseignement Mathematique: une Approach Socio-Cognitive, quoted in Mitsikopoulou, V. (1988) *Writing with a Word Processor.* Unpublished thesis submitted for the specialist diploma in Microcomputers in Education, University of London Institute of Education.

Barbieri, M. S. and Light, P. (1992) Interaction, gender and performance on a computer-based problem solving task. *Learning and Instruction,* 2, 199–214.

Barnard, Y. and Sandberg, J. (1992) Interviews on AI and Education: Beverly Woolf and Roger Shank. *AICOM,* 5, 148–155.

Baskerville, J. (1986) The language curriculum and the role of word processors in developing written language in the primary school. In Trushell, J. (ed.) *A Word Processor in the Language Classroom.* Slough, Berks: National Foundation for Educational Research.

Bennett, J.P. (1991) Effectiveness of the computer in the teaching of secondary school mathematics: Fifteen years of reviews of research. *Educational Technology,* **Aug.,** 44–47.

Beynon, J. (1993) Computers, dominant boys and invisible girls: or, 'Hannah, it's not a toaster, it's a computer!" In Beynon, J. and Mackay, H. *Computers into Classrooms: More Questions than Answers.* London: Falmer Press.

Bransford, J., Franks, J., Vye, N. and Sherwood, R. (1989) New approaches to instruction: Because wisdom can't be told. In Vosniadou, S. and Ortony, A. (eds.) *Similarity and Analogical Reasoning.* New York: Cambridge University Press.

Brent Micro-Technology Education Centre (1988) *The Word Processing and Language Development Project.* London: Brent Education Department.

Brown, J. and Howlett, F. (1994) *IT Works.* Coventry: NCET.

Clark, M. (1984) Young writers and the computer. In Chandler, D and Marcus S. (eds) *Computers and Literacy.* Milton Keynes: Open University Press.

Clark, R.E. (1983) Reconsidering research on learning from media. *Review of Educational Research,* 4, 445–459.

Claxton, G. (1991) *Educating the Inquiring Mind.* London: Harvester Wheatsheaf.

Cochrane-Smith, M. (1991) Word processing and writing in elementary classrooms: a critical review of related literature. *Review of Educational Research,* 61(1), 104–105.

Collis B.A. (1992) Supporting educational uses of telecommunications in secondary school: Part 1 analysis of experience. *International Journal for Instructional Media,* 19(1).

Collis B.A. (1993) Evaluating instructional applications of telecommunications in distance education. *Education Training Technologies International,* 30(3), 266–274.

Cooper, M. (1990) *Electronic 'Paint' – A New Medium In Art Education.* Coventry: NCET.

Coyle, D. and Harrison, C. (1993) The EHE-EMSAT Project: the development of awareness of electronic mail among student teachers. *Journal of Information Technology in Teacher Education,* 2(1), 89–103.

Culley, L. (1988) Girls, boys and computers. *Educational Studies,* 14, 3–8.

Daiute, C. (1986) *Writing and Computers.* Reading, Massachusetts: Addison-Wesley.

Davis N.E. (1988) Supporting professional development with Information Technology networks. *Programmed Learning and Educational Technology,* 24(4), 344–347.

166

Davis N.E. (1993) Border crossings. *Times Educational Supplement*, **1 Jan,** 24.
Davis N.E. (1994) ISDN technology in teaching. In Mason,R. and Bacsich, P. (eds) *ISDN Applications In Education And Training*. London: Institute of Electrical Engineers.
Dearing, R. (1993) *The National Curriculum and its Assessment. Interim Report*. London: HMSO.
de Bono (1983) *Atlas of Management Thinking*. Harmondsworth, Middlesex: Penguin.
DES (1988) *English for Ages 5 to 11*. London: HMSO.
DES (1989a) *English for Ages 5 to 16*. London: HMSO.
DES (1989b) *Design and Technology for Ages 5 to 16*. London: HMSO.
DES (1990) *Technology in the National Curriculum*. London: HMSO.
DES (1991) *Science in the National Curriculum*. London: HMSO.
DES(1992) *Art in the National Curriculum*. London: HMSO.
DES, (1991) *Science in the National Curriculum*. London: HMSO.
DFE, (1992) *Information Technology in Secondary Schools – A review by HMI*. London: HMSO.
DFE (1993) *Survey of Information Technology in Schools: Statistical Bulletin 6/93*. London: HMSO.
Digital Image(1992) *Computer Graphics Art Work, Graphic-Sha*. Japan.
Earl, S. (1987) Let's make a book with Writer. *Microscope*, **21**, 3–7.
Emig, J. (1982) *Writing Composition and Rhetoric. Vol. 2: Language and Literacy*. Milton Keynes: Open University Press.
Fitzpatrick, H. and Hardman, M. (1993) Girls, boys and the classroom computer: an equal partnership? *Paper presented at the meeting of Developmental Psychology Section of British Psychological Society, Birmingham*, September.
Freedman and Pringle (1989) Unpublished observations.
Gallagher B. (1985) Microcomputers and word processing programs: an evaluation and critique. Research Monograph, Series Report No. 9. Quoted in Mitsikpoulou, V. (1988) *Writing with a Word Processor*. Unpublished thesis submitted for the specialist diploma in Microcomputers in Education, University of London Institute of Education.
Graves D. (1982) *Writing: Teachers and Children at Work*. London: Heinemann.
Green, J. (1984) Computers, Kids and Writing: An Interview with Donald Graves. *Classroom Computer Learning*, **4** , 20–22.
Hammond, M. (1993a) *Handling Data with Spreadsheets and Databases in Science*. Sheffield: The Centre for Statistical Education, University of Sheffield.
Hammond, M. (1993b) *Handling Data with Databases and Spreadsheets. A Classroom Pack*. London: Hodder and Stoughton.
Healy, L. and Sutherland, R. (1991) *Exploring Mathematics with Spreadsheets*. London: Simon and Schuster Education.
HMI (1992) *Information Technology in Secondary Schools*. London: HMSO.
Hodgson, A. *et al.* (1993) *Information Technology in Design Technology: A discussion paper*. Department of Design and Technology, Loughborough Unversity of Technology.
Howe, C., Tolmie, A. and Anderson, A. (1991) Information technology and group work in physics. *Journal of Computer Assisted Learning*, **7**, 133–143.
Hoyles, C. (1988) *Girls and Computers*, Bedford Way Papers, 34, London: Institute of Education, University of London.
Hughes, M. and Greenhough, P. (1989) Gender and social interaction in early LOGO use. In: Collins, J. H., Estes, N., Gattis, W. D., and Walker, D. (eds). *The Sixth International Conference on Technology and Education, Vol. 1*. Edinburgh: CEP.
Joiner, R. (1993) *A Dialogue Model of the Resolution of Inter-Individual Conflicts: Implications for Computer Based Collaborative Learning*. PhD Thesis, The Open University.
Keeling, R. and Whiteman, S. (1990) *Simply Spreadsheets*, KW Publications.
Kemmis, S.. Atkin, R. and Wright, E. (1977) *How Do Students Learn? Working Papers On CAL*. Norwich: Centre for Applied Research in Education, UEA.
Klahr, D. and Carver, S. M. (1988) Cognitive objectives in a LOGO debugging curriculum: instruction, learning and transfer. *Cognitive Psychology*, **20**, 362–404.
Kruger, A. C. (1993) Peer collaboration: conflict, co-operation or both? *Social*

Development, **2,** 165–182.

Lave, J. and Wenger, E. (1991) *Situated Learning: Legitimate Peripheral Participation.* Cambridge: Cambridge University Press.

Leicester University (1992) *INSIGHT Data-Logging Software.* Cambridge: Longman Logotron.

Light, P. and Mavarech, Z. (1992) Co-operative learning with computers and introduction. *Learning and Instruction,* **2,** 155–159.

Littleton, K., Light, P., Barnes, P., Messer, D. and Joiner, R. (1993) Gender and software effects in computer-based problem solving. *Paper presented at the Society for Research in Child Development,* New Orleans, March.

Malone, B. (1987) Using a word processor to teach children to read. *Paper presented at the MAPE Conference,* April.

Marcus S. and Blau, S (1983) Not Sweeing is Relieving: Invisible Writing with Computers. *Educational Technology,* **April,**12–15.

Martin, N., *et al.* (1976) *Writing and Language Across the Curriculum 11–16.* London: Ward Lock.

Meadows, J. (1992) International collaborations in teacher education: a constructivist approach to using electronic mail for communication in partnership with schools. *Journal of Information Technology in Teacher Education,* **1(1),** 113-125.

NATE (1991) *IT's English.* Sheffield: National Association for the Teaching of English.

National Writing Project (1990) *Writing and Micros.* Walton-on-Thames: Nelson/SCDC Publications.

NCET (1993) *Evaluation of IT in Science.* Coventry: NCET.

Nelson, R. (undated) Word processing with children. In Birmingham Micro Group *Computer Uses in English.* Birmingham: Educational Computing Centre.

Olson, D. (1986) Intelligence and literacy: The relationship between intelligence and the technologies of representation and communication. In Sternberg, R.J. and Wagner,R.K. (eds). *Practical Intelligence: Nature and Origins of Competence in the Everyday World.* Cambridge: Cambridge University Press.

Olson, J. (1988) *Schoolworlds – Microworlds.* Oxford: Pergamon.

Opie, I. and Opie, P. (1969) *Children's Games In Street And Playground.* Oxford: Oxford University Press.

Owen, M. (1993) Schools in control?: questions about the development of the teaching of cybernetics. *Paper presented at IDATER 93, Loughborough University of Technology.*

Papert, S. (1980) *Mindstorms: Children, Computers and Powerful Ideas.* New York: Harvester Press.

Papert, S. (1994) *The Children's Machine.* Hemel Hemstead:Harvester Wheatsheaf.

Pea, R. (1985) Beyond amplification: Using the computer to reorganise mental functioning. *Educational Psychologist,* **20,** 167–182.

Peacock, M. (1987) *The Writing Tool: Secondary Pupils' Use of and Response to the Computer as a Word Processor.* Unpublished paper. Sheffield University: Division of Education.

Peasey, D. (1985) Using spreadsheet programs in mathematics education. *Micromath,* **1,** 44–46.

Perkins, D. (1992) Technology meets constructivism: Do they make a marriage? In Duffy, T. and Jonassen, D. (eds) *Constructivism and the Technology of Instruction: A Conversation.* New Jersey: Lawrence Erlbaum Associates.

Piaget, J. (1952) *The Origins of Intelligence in Young Children.* New York: IUP.

Piaget, J. (1982) *The Child's Conception of the World.* London: Palladin.

Potter, F. (1988a) The word processor: a new literacy tool. Paper presented at *CEC Summer University on Writing and First Contacts with Written Language,* University of Toulouse le Mirail, July.

Potter, F. (1988b) Word processing and literacy skills; an outline of our current state of knowledge. Paper given at the seminar *'New Information Technologies and Literacy Skills: Applications and Implications for Reading and Writing'* held at Edge Hill College of Higher Education, Ormskirk, July.

Pullinger, D. and Wellavize, D. (1984) *An Experiment into Reading Journal Articles on Screen.* Report to the British National Bibliographic Research Fund on Project SI/BRG/48.

168

Ragsdale, R. (1991) Effective computing in education: teachers, tools and training. *Education and Computing*, **7**, 157–166.

Rogers, L. and Barton, R. *Information Technology in School Science*. Unpublished document, University of Leicester.

Rogers, L.T. (1992) *Insight Measurement Software: Teachers' Guide*. Cambridge: Longman Logotron.

Rogers, L.T. and Wild, P. (1993) *The Use Of I.T. in Practical Science – A Study in Three Schools*. Leicester: Leicester University.

Said, A. (1993) The effectiveness of using pre-prepared electronic spreadsheet and the students' attutudes towards its use in mathematics tutorial classes. *Computer Education*, **Nov**, 6–9.

Salomon, G. (1990) Cognitive effects with and of computer technologies. *Communication Research*, **17**, 26–44.

Schutz, A. (1982) *Life Forms and Meaning Structure*. Translated, introduced and annotated by Wagner, H. London: Routledge & Kegan Paul.

Scrimshaw, P. (ed.) (1993) *Language, Classrooms and Computers*. London: Routledge.

Smith, F. (1991) *IT's English*. Sheffield: National Association for the Teaching of English.

Somekh, B. (1986) Exploring word processing with children. In Trushell, J. (ed.) *A Word Processor in the Language Classroom*. Slough, Berks: National Foundation for Educational Research.

Sudol, R. (1985) Applied word processing: Notes on authority, responsibility and revision in a workshop model. *College Composition and Communication*, 36(3), October, 331–335.

Suppes, P. (1966) The uses of computers in education. *Scientific American*, **215**, 207–220.

Sweetman, J. (1993) *Curriculum Confidential 4*. Lemington Spa: Courseware Publications.

Szymanski, Sunal, Sunal and Sheffler (1993) Communications technology in the classroom – exploring implications for teacher education: a case study. *Journal of Technology and Teacher Education*, 1(3), 275–289

Trushell, J. (ed.) (1986) *A Word Processor in the Language Classroom*. Slough, Berks.: National Foundation for Educational Research.

Underwood, J. (1986). The role of the computer in developing children's classificatory abilities. *Computers and Education*, **10**, 175–180.

Underwood, J. and Underwood, G. (1987) Data retrieval and organisation by children. *British Journal of Educational Psychology*, **57**, 313–329.

Underwood, J. and Underwood, G. (1990). *Computers and Learning: Helping Children Acquire Thinking Skills*. Oxford: Blackwells.

Underwood, G., McCaffrey, M. and Underwood, J. (1990). Gender differences in a co-operative computer-based language task. *Educational Research*, **32**, 44–49.

Underwood, G., Underwood, J. and Turner, M. (1993). Children's thinking during collaborative computer-based problem solving. *Educational Psychology*, **13**, 345–357.

Underwood, G., Jindal, N. and Underwood, J. (1994). Gender differences and effects of co-operation in a computer-based language task. *Educational Research*, **36**, 63–74.

Vygotsky, L. (1978) *Mind In Society: The Development of Higher Psychological Processes*. Cambridge, MA. Harvard University Press.

Welsh Office (1992) *Survey of the Use of Information Technology in the Secondary Schools of Wales*. London: HMSO.

Whalley, P. (1992) Making control technology work in the classroom. *British Journal of Educational Technology*, 23(3), 212–221.

Wishart, J. and Canter, D. (1988) Variations in user involvement with educational software. *Computers and Education*, **12**, 365–379.

Wood, D. J. (1988) *How Children Think and Learn*. Oxford: Blackwells.

Woolnough, B.E. (1991) *Practical Science*. Milton Keynes: Open University Press.

Index